# COLLECTING ANTIQUES
# FOR THE FUTURE

# COLLECTING ANTIQUES FOR THE FUTURE

## Joan Bamford

LUTTERWORTH PRESS
Richard Smart Publishing

First published 1976

Published by Lutterworth Press
Luke House, Farnham Road, Guildford, Surrey
and Richard Smart Publishing
Copyright © Joan Bamford, 1976
ISBN 0 7188 7008 5
Printed by Jolly & Barber Ltd
Rugby, Warwickshire

# CONTENTS

# ILLUSTRATIONS

To my husband, Jack
With love and appreciation for his help and encouragement

# ACKNOWLEDGMENTS

First and foremost I should like to thank the following artist–craftsmen, antique dealers and good friends concerned who have kindly lent me the photographs to illustrate this book. The credits are given in the order that the photographs appear in each chapter.

*Chapter 1.* 1 and 2 by Francis Butters, courtesy of the Worshipful Company of Goldsmiths, London. 3, 4, 5 and 6 Stuart Devlin, London, EC1.

*Chapter 2.* 1–5 Worcester Royal Porcelain Company, Ltd. 6 Robert Fish, California. 7 Pinckney Photography, California.

*Chapter 3.* 1 Beryl Dean. 2 The Dean and Canons of Windsor. 3, 4 and 5 Hastings Corporation. 6 Margaret Kaye, London.

*Chapter 4.* 1 Christie's, London. 2 and 3 Peter Dreiser. 4 Stuart and Sons Ltd, Stourbridge. 5 Strathearn Glass, Ltd.

*Chapter 5.* 1 and 3 Craft Advisory Committee. 2 Bernard Leach. 4 British Craft Centre, Waterloo Place, London, SW1. 5 Michael Casson.

*Chapter 6.* 1 Richard Ogden. 2 Worshipful Company of Goldsmiths. 3 and 4 De Beers, London. 5 N. Bloom and Son and De Beers, London. 6, 7 and 8 Cameo Corner, London, WC1. 9 Worshipful Company of Goldsmiths.

*Chapter 7.* 1 Wedgwood and Sons Ltd. 2 Doulton and Co Ltd. 3 and 4 Wedgwood and Sons Ltd. 5, 6 and 7 Wolverhampton Art Gallery and Museum. 9 and 10 Wedgwood and Sons Ltd.

*Chapter 8.* 1 Private Loan Exhibition. 2 Chelsea Antiques Fair. 3 Frank Staff. 4 Hallmark Cards. 5 Knight, Frank and Rutley. 6 Stirling Health, England.

*Chapter 9.* 2 Bruford and Carr, London, W1. 3 Cameo Corner, London, WC1. 4 Private Loan Exhibition, Chelsea Antiques Fair. 5 Author's collection.

*Chapter 10.* 1 Maple Antiques, London. 3 Phillips Auctioneers, Blenheim Street, London, W1. 4 Design Centre, Haymarket, London. 5 Christie's, London, SW1. 6 W. R. Harvey and Co, London, NW3. 8 Worshipful Company of Goldsmiths.

*Chapter 11.* 1 Whitefriars Glass, England. 2 Sotheby and Co, London, W1. 5 Council for Industrial Design, London.

*Chapter 12.* 1 and 2 Crispin, St Albans. 4 Phillips Auctioneers, Blenheim Street, London, W1. 5 Reckitt and Colman, Norwich. 6 and 7 Chelsea Antiques Fair, and Divertimenti, Marylebone Lane, London, NW1.

*Chapter 13.* 3 John Waddington Playing Card Company. 6 Phillips Auctioneers, Blenheim Street, London, W1. 7 Sotheby and Co, London, W1.

*Chapter 14.* 1, 2 and 3 Chelsea Antiques Fair. 5 Council for Industrial Design, London.

*Chapter 15.* 1 Baynton-Williams, London, SW1. 2 Crispin, St Albans. 3 Waterways Museum, Stoke Bruerne. 4 Knight, Frank and Rutley. 5 Baynton-Williams, London, SW1. 6 Vauxhall Ltd, Luton. 7 Christie's, London, SW1.

*Chapter 16.* 1 and 2 Christopher Sykes, Woburn, Bedfordshire. 3 Aspreys, Bond Street, London, W1. 5 Halcyon Days Ltd, Brook Street, London, SW1.

I should also like to express my great appreciation to Bernard Price for so kindly writing the Foreword, and for his good wishes and kindness. My special thanks are also due to Richard Smart. Also my very real thanks are certainly due to Mrs Prudence Hannay who has typed with patience and skill the manuscript from my enthusiastic but often almost illegible writing. To these and also to so many other good friends such as John Bly who have given me encouragement to carry this idea through to a tangible result, I should like to express my affectionate and very real apreciation.

Above all, I should like to send my greetings to the readers of this book. I hope that they may find something to help and encourage them in their interest in beautiful and fascinating items of which there is such an abundance in the world around us.

# FOREWORD

Books on antiques and collecting continue to flow from the publishing houses in an effort to both satisfy and stimulate the wide public interest in such subjects. This book, however, is different to most. It does not set out to describe in any detail the great works of the past. Neither does it pretend to instruct the reader in techniques of identification in separating original work from the copy or outright fake. Instead, Joan Bamford has written a well illustrated and timely volume that reminds us that all fine things are by no means restricted to the antique and that craftsmanship in no way vanished with the crowning of Queen Victoria.

Attention is also drawn to the way in which once common objects of everyday life grow in importance as they punctuate the changes that have occurred over the last one hundred momentous years. For the real collector we see how rich the opportunities are, and the importance and satisfaction of collecting only the best examples you can find.

For many people it takes far more courage to collect from the present than it does to search among the past, and I hope that this book may give fresh confidence. Obviously there are gaps and omissions in the book, how could it be otherwise in a subject that demonstrates so well the continuing thread that links and makes whole the words and deeds of the past, present and future. Having known and respected Joan Bamford and her work for at least a decade, it gives me particular pleasure to wish her book well, and all those who read it.

BERNARD PRICE

# INTRODUCTION

What is an antique? My Pocket Oxford Dictionary states: 'Dating from old times: in the manner of the ancients: old-fashioned: a relic, especially a work of art.'

According to Customs Regulations the ruling is that to be regarded as an antique the object must have been made one hundred years ago. This convention is also used generally by the antiques trade. In fact some dealers in quality goods, especially furniture, stop at 1830 with the death of George IV, regarded in 'the history of taste' as the end of an era. However, while one hundred years old has become generally recognised for most articles sold at Antiques Fairs, the date for pictures, jewellery, carpets and several other categories is not so strictly judged.

As the demand for collectables grows, Victoriana of all kinds is becoming more popular. The antiques of earlier periods have become scarcer and the collector has to look for fresh fields. So why not look to the present for interesting and well-made objects which will surely be the antiques of the future? While looking back in the art world is delightful for a collector, looking forward can be as rewarding.

In this book we hope to present many ideas for future collections. A hundred years from now antiques will include the fine work of some of our present-day artists and craftsmen whose talents measure up to famous names from the past, but whose work is in what we think of as 'the modern idiom'. Without doubt the 1960s and 70s have brought to light a fresh creative spirit in the arts and the crafts.

In addition to looking forward with some of today's craftsmen, the book also suggests some simple collectables belonging to the last hundred years or so which in their own right are also antiques for the future.

J.B.

# PART I  TODAY'S TREASURES

# 1 TWENTIETH-CENTURY HEIRLOOMS

The finest craftsmen and designers in any age inevitably reflect the spirit of their own times, and this is certainly true of the work of some present-day gold- and silversmiths whose masterpieces have the qualities that will surely carry them forward to become 'Antiques for the Future'.

Throughout the centuries artist-craftsmen have created beautiful objects in gold and silver, and the durability of these precious metals has given their work a high rate of survival.

The strict hall-marking laws in Britain have long provided a recognised status and interest for gold and silverware made in this country. These laws were introduced six and a half centuries ago and they have continued to safeguard articles made of gold and sterling silver ever since. They also act as the oldest form of consumer protection in the world as it is still illegal to sell British-made silver and gold objects unless they are marked to indicate the maker, place, date and purity of the piece in the required manner. This is a great help to the collector who can arm himself with one of the reliable books on hallmarks now available.

Much of the credit for the fine reputation held by British silverware is due to the famous Worshipful Company of Goldsmiths, founded in London in the Middle Ages, whose activities over the centuries, have set and upheld the highest standards for all craftsmen.

It would be quite impossible in the limited space of this book to mention the many fine artist-craftsmen designing and making silverware today, whose creative abilities will make their work collectable for future generations. We have therefore selected just two of these as examples of outstanding vision and skill; they are truly representative of some of the finest present-day craftsmen, whose work will one day rank as valuable antiques. Collectors of today's treasures may well select the work of other fine artists whose designs also express the spirit of this era, and have that living quality in their work that shares an ageless language.

It has been said that 'Louis Osman's wonderful creative vitality speaks for itself'. It is certainly conveyed through his work. In addition to his being a superb and experienced silversmith and jeweller, he is a qualified architect and archaeologist and has won many awards. His hall-mark was registered at Goldsmiths' Hall, London, in 1958, and much of his work is now in public and private collections, and can also be seen in churches and cathedrals in Britain and elsewhere. He was responsible for designing and making the crown for the Prince of Wales at his Investiture at Caernarvon Castle in 1969, which may well be the only crown made in this century.

This important piece of work was commissioned by the Worshipful Company of Goldsmiths who were privileged to present it to the Queen. It was made at Louis Osman's workshops at Canons Ashby in the countryside between Banbury and Northampton, and he co-ordinated the work of many specialists and expert advisers (including his wife, Dylis) in creating this historic crown. His wide experience enabled him to evolve this lovely masterpiece which combines simplicity with a restrained splendour – a national treasure appropriate to the occasion and skilfully representing the spirit of our times whilst preserving its heirloom qualities.

The design is symbolic and makes the most of the piece's historic associations. It can be seen to comprise an integral circle and single arch of 24-carat gold, electro-formed from Mr Osman's wax original. Around the circle of the crown are four-forged crosses, each built up from four 'nails' of 22-carat Welsh gold, reinforced with iridium platinum, and held at the centres with a reinforcing motif of four small irregularly

1. *and* 2. Above, *the crown Louis Osman designed and made specially for the Investiture of the Prince of Wales at Caernarvon Castle in 1969, and for use at all future investitures of the Princes of Wales.* Below, *Louis Osman at work on the crown*

placed square-cut diamonds. There is a further square-cut diamond set in platinum at the end of each arm of the cross. Four fleurs de lys, each formed in 22-carat Welsh gold, are reinforced with iridium platinum and are held by three square-cut emeralds in gold settings. The green emeralds echo the Welsh national colour.

Although a small gold circlet was made for the investiture of the young Prince Edward, later known as the Duke of Windsor it seems that any other crowns made for the Princes of Wales since the fourteenth century have long since been lost. It therefore makes the present crown a specially important piece of work appropriate for future investitures of the Prince Paramount in his Principality of Wales.

The orb on this crown,* suggesting the world and worldly influences, is engraved with the wearer's attributes; the Dragon of Wales; the Lion of England and the early Princes of Wales; the Unicorn of Scotland; corn stooks of the Earl of Chester; feathers of the Prince of Wales and also the Black Prince; bezants of the Duke of Cornwall. Superimposed diamond stars are arranged in the shape of Scorpio (Prince Charles was born in November) and suggest space; seven stones suggest the seven deadly sins and the seven gifts from God under the domination of the Cross. The Cross symbolises Christian, spiritual power; the crosses round the side protection, and the fleurs de lys purity. There are in all seventy-five square diamonds of tiny size, and twelve square emeralds; it was decided that a show of huge stones would be out of keeping with today's duty-bound monarchy, but the sparkle of these small stones relieves the soft peach sheen of the burnished but unpolished gold.

The main body of the crown carries the London Assay Office hall-marks for 22-carat gold; the maker's mark L.O., for Louis Osman; the standard mark for gold – a crown; the 22-carat mark; the London Assay Office mark – a leopard's

---

*The traditional orb on early crowns represented an apple, the symbol of original sin.

head and the date letter 'O' showing that it was completed between mid-May 1969 and mid-May 1970.

We have described this piece of Louis Osman's work in detail as being a specially interesting and historic piece giving great scope for his artist's vision and craftsman's skill. His jewellery, presentation pieces and ecclesiastical plate, however, are all unique (he does not do any but individual pieces, especially designed for particular persons, places and associations) and he refuses to use any mechanical processes in production so that all his work will mellow and improve as it patinates with age, use and handling.

These pieces are all of the highest quality and so of timeless interest, whether they are formed from thick earthy pieces of gold, or from paper-thin webs set with sparkling stones or lustrous pearls. Louis Osman's technical skill has contributed much to encourage other artist-craftsmen in their constant search for perfection.

Today's treasures designed and made by Stuart Devlin, the Australian silversmith and jeweller, of outstanding talent, will also surely become fabulous antiques in the future.

His highly individualistic work makes it easily recognisable, even though there are now so many other gifted young silversmiths working in the modern idiom that a whole volume could be filled with accounts of their activities and achievements. The 1960s and 70s will surely be remembered for the work of many fine artist-craftsmen, and it seems likely that it will be recalled as a time of general renaissance in the arts and crafts.

Stuart Devlin's success has been achieved by his remarkable ability to develop new and varied ideas. His wide experience and capacity for hard work have made it possible for him to translate these into gold and silver objects of great originality and beauty. It is his technical mastery that enabled him to instil, in the precious metals, the magic of his imagination. His designs are mostly inspired by nature as can be seen in the textures of the gold and silver, reminiscent of the rough bark of trees, the sparkling ripples of water, sunlight through leaves, and other natural objects. He also uses the human form in action, as in his tiny caryatic figures supporting goblets or radiating from precious stones in the settings of his exquisite jewellery.

His famous Surprise Eggs made in either silver or gold filagree, contain either an uncut piece of semi-precious stone or a gem-stone with interesting facets. These are all treasured heirloom pieces. The gold and silver he uses to form the age-old shape of eggs and the stones these fabulous toys contain, may have lain deep within the earth's surface for thousands or millions of years, linking the far distant past with the skills of the present day artist-craftsman.

*3. A range of Stuart Devlin's famous Surprise Eggs in gold and silver, some opened to display their 'surprise'*

4. *Hand-raised silver wine goblets by Stuart Devlin for white wine, champagne and claret*

Stuart Devlin, born in Geelong, Australia, knew at the age of fourteen, when he won his first scholarship to the London Institute of Technology, that he wanted to be a designer, and he has never deviated from that ambition. This talented artist-craftsman has been winning diplomas, scholarships and prizes ever since, both in art and technology.

Having studied at the Royal Melbourne Institute of Technology where he won the highest marks ever awarded after only one year's study instead of the usual three, he was also awarded three scholarships which brought him to the Royal College of Art in London. Here he studied Light Engineering Design, and gold and silver-smithing, and left as the only student ever to obtain honours diplomas in both subjects. He also won the Thesis Prize for that year. He spent the next two years in America on yet another travel award, the Harkness Fellowship, and he was there provided with his own studio. During this time, he studied and lectured at many universities. He also developed his interest in sculpture and held a one-man exhibition of his own work at the Thibaut Gallery in New York, and in 1965 at the Terry Clune Gallery in Sydney.

On his return to Australia Stuart Devlin was awarded his first major commission – to design Australia's decimal coinage which was recognised as a fine and appropriate piece of work.

This was an important turning point in his life as he had to return to London to supervise his designs which were carried out at the Mint. While in London he and his American wife, Kim, decided to make goldsmithing their life and London their home, and there they continue to work together as partners. They chose Clerkenwell, by long tradition a silver-smithing area, for their home and workshop. Their windows overlook part of the old monastery garden near St John's Gate into the City – a delightful background to the workshops, where now a number of apprentices are qualifying to become competent silversmiths. Stuart Devlin has done much to raise the standing of the craftsmen who work for him and it has now been accepted that some pieces made in the Stuart Devlin

5. *Stuart Devlin's first major commission, designing Australia's decimal coinage. The designs are: 1 cent, a Feather-tail Glider, 2 cents, a Frill-necked Lizard. 5 cents, an Echnida (or Spiny Ant-eater). 10 cents, a Lyre Bird. 20 cents, a Platypus. 50 cents, the coat of arms*

workshops after 1973 can carry a Master-Mark in addition to the usual Hall-Marks. A Master-Mark is awarded to a craftsman when he has been elected by his peers to the status of Master Craftsman and indicates that through training and experience, he is able to produce exceptional work in his special branch of the craft. This mark can now be used at the discretion of the craftsman concerned and indicates that the piece can reasonably be termed 'a masterpiece'. Eight of the craftsmen now working in the Devlin workshops have qualified for this distinction.

In the years that Stuart Devlin has been working in the United Kingdom he has designed and made many important presentation trophies as well as the fabulous silverware and the spectacularly beautiful objets d'art so sought by connoisseur collectors, and these in addition to countless privately commissioned pieces of gold, silver and jewellery.

6. *A special commission by Stuart Devlin, a hand-raised 18-carat green gold christening cup decorated with hand-made gold figures*

In 1966 he was made a Freeman of the Worshipful Company of Goldsmiths who acclaim him as 'the designer with the Midas touch', and they honoured him again in 1972 by electing him a Liveryman, so it is not surprising that collectors of his original work in gold, silver and precious stones, consider themselves fortunate indeed to possess treasures with such fabulous lasting qualities.

# 2 PORCELAIN MASTERPIECES

Since the art of porcelain-making first became known in Europe some 250 years ago, ceramic sculpture has developed in the hands of a number of very fine artist-craftsmen and women, and some of their work equals (if not surpasses) models made by the famous J. J. Kaendler at Meissen in the 18th century which now fetches such vast sums on the rare occasions it comes up for sale at auctions.

Dorothy Doughty, for example, working for the Worcester Royal Porcelain Company, has justly been called one of the greatest modellers in porcelain of our time, and her famous series of American and British birds and flowers are now eagerly sought collector's pieces on both sides of the Atlantic and beyond.

All her models are made in limited editions of five hundred or less, and when an edition is completed, the moulds are destroyed. The rarity of the models increases their value and this, together with the quality of the work, guarantees it a place among the fabulous antiques of the future.

Miss Doughty was a worker of wide experience and tremendous energy and she made several series of models before her untimely death in 1962. Her work now has a special scarcity value and when it changes hands is eagerly sought out by connoisseur collectors. Happily, Worcester Royal Porcelain Company still have some of her completed bird models which they have not yet issued, and from time to time, as much as several years apart, these are brought out in strictly limited editions.

Her many bird models were always made with the appropriate flowers or trees as she felt they were inseparable. Her treatment was entirely her own, although she never tired of paying tribute to the fine team of craftsmen and women whose skill and patience overcame the enormous difficulties of translating her life-like models into permanent forms, a fine art in itself. Their work combined with her inspiration and skilled modelling, has led to there being a talented group at the Worcester Royal Porcelain Company who are specially skilled in the many technical difficulties involved when making birds, flowers, and foliage so close to nature.

Dorothy Doughty was a keen amateur ornithologist and naturalist, and during World War II, when the porcelain industry in this country was at a very low ebb, a proposal was made to the historic Worcester Royal Porcelain Company by Alex Dickens, an art dealer, that they might make a series of American bird models in porcelain, using a surface nearer to nature than the usual high glaze porcelain. The outcome of this suggestion was that they asked Dorothy Doughty to undertake this work on their behalf and she began by sketching American birds in museums and working from real flowers and foliage sent to her from The Royal Botanical Gardens at Kew. Her flower models were the most exact reproductions yet attempted in porcelain of a living plant, and by 1940 she was earning vital dollars despite shortages and increasingly frequent attacks by enemy aircraft. In what leisure time she had from her ambulance work and other wartime activities she continued the series of American birds.

In 1943 she and her family moved to Falmouth, in Cornwall, where she installed an aviary so that she could work from living bird models, and she also built a small kiln in the garden for experimental firings of her models.

The abundant wild flowers and bird life in the area were a renewed inspiration and she resolved that one day she would also make a series of British birds with their appropriate wild flowers, an ambition that happily she fulfilled at a later date.

1. *Dorothy Doughty's Chiffchaff on Hogweed modelled in the West of England in summer. The delicacy of the plant life was part of her genius*

In 1953, with the war in Europe over, she travelled to America on behalf of the Worcester Royal Porcelain Company, and there she spent nearly three months sketching birds from life for yet another series of American birds to meet the great demand for her work. She again crossed the Atlantic in 1956 and this time went to Texas, New Mexico and Arizona where the birds and foliage were different and presented fresh problems. She was a perfectionist who refused to compromise in her work and her models are accurate representations in size, colour and background, of the living birds and plants on which she worked.

In 1957 when Her Majesty the Queen visited the United States, she presented President Eisenhower with a pair of Dorothy Doughty's Parula Warblers – a most appropriate gift which was greatly appreciated.

Her birds seldom come up for sale today but when they do they fetch fabulous sums. For example, in March 1973 Sotheby's of Belgravia were able to include in an important sale of English ceramics some examples of the American birds modelled by Dorothy Doughty and from her personal collection. This collection included finished pieces of the porcelain groups she had designed for the Worcester Royal Porcelain Company under the terms of her Agreement with them. From this sale is illustrated opposite a Cactus Wren, one of a pair, perched amid prickly pears. The pair fetched £3,200.

A pair of these delightful and world-famous birds, modelled in 1940, has the privilege of being amongst the most heavily insured pieces in the well-known Dyson Perrins Museum of Royal Worcester Porcelain. It is estimated to be even more valuable than some of the great pieces made in this historic manufactory during the famous Dr Wall* period. This fabulous exhibit is a pair of Bob White Quails. (We understand that a similar pair changed hands at auction in the United States a few years ago at $50,000.)

*A factory was founded at Worcester in 1751 and in 1752 incorporated the Bristol factory. The period 1751–83 is known as the 'Dr Wall' period.

*2. One of Dorothy Doughty's famous American birds, a Cactus Wren perched amid prickly pears, from her personal collection*

Specimens of her British birds can be seen at this museum in Worcester. The more recent models are sometimes on view and for sale in London at more reasonable prices at Thomas Goode and Company of South Audley Street, also at Harrods of Knightsbridge and Asprey's of Bond Street.

The life-like texture of the glaze she used, the accuracy of colour, and above all the sense of life and movement she captured in her models make them rare treasures. Many porcelain modellers coming after her have copied her methods, some fairly successfully, but the exquisite quality of her work which was wrought with love and understanding is unique.

Doris Lindner is another celebrated artist and ceramic sculptor whose life-like animal portrait models, now world famous, are carried out in superb quality Royal Worcester porcelain. She specialises in individual portraits of famous horses and prize bulls and travels to America and many other parts of the world, when commissioned, to model her subjects from life. These models are all issued in strictly limited editions. They are seldom re-sold at present but when they do change hands, they are found to have considerably increased in value, and without doubt they will be considered as valuable antiques in the years to come.

Her skilful fine porcelain animal portraits combine a living quality with such a perfect representation that they are recognised by breed societies for their complete accuracy. They will undoubtedly survive the years.

Doris Lindner has also worked in stone, wood, concrete and bronze and has successfully exhibited her work in the Royal Academy and elsewhere. She has said that stone is really her favourite medium because of its creative possibilities which give her great satisfaction. To illustrate this point there is the story of a small boy watching fascinated as a sculptor was cutting away at a huge block of stone. As a lion's head gradually began to emerge he asked: 'How did you know there was a lion in that stone?'

Doris Lindner's studio is in Chipping Campden, an area of lovely Cotswold stone houses, farms and cottages where she has the joy of seeing horses and farm animals as part of the everyday scene.

She always returns to animals in her work and achieves a remarkable sense of life and movement, the vigour of her models expressing her own lively personality. As she puts it herself, she loves 'the majesty of prize bulls, stallions and race horses'.

Her famous animal portraits are meticulously carried out in finest porcelain by the highly skilled team of craftsmen and painters at Royal Worcester. They use a particular glaze, quite

3. *Doris Lindner travels the world making portraits of horses and bulls in ceramic sculpture. Here she is modelling a prize Braham bull on a Texas ranch*

unlike a high gloss finish, which enhances the life-like quality of the model and is one of its special charms.

For her work Doris Lindner travels widely and makes careful models in the animals' home surroundings. She sketches from life, uses a camera and translates her first findings into a preliminary clay model. She greatly enjoys the travelling necessitated by this work which has taken her to various parts of Europe, the United States, Canada, France and Ireland. She has never lacked courage and is fearless where animals are concerned, remaining quite undisturbed however formidable her model may be. (See illustration above.)

As a young girl she took up flying and gained an 'A' Licence, and during World War II she drove an ambulance in the London blitz. Race meetings and driving still give her great enjoyment, but she says that the peace and tranquillity of her 250 year-old Cotswold cottage provide the best place to work in and she loves to be where so many of her friends and neighbours are artists or craftsmen. City life no longer appeals to her.

There have been many famous animals among her models, and perhaps the most widely known of these is 'Tommy', the horse in the fine equestrian portrait of the Queen when, as Princess Elizabeth, she took the salute on behalf of her father, King George VI at the Trooping of the Colour.

This model was made at the special wish of Her Majesty Queen Elizabeth, the Queen Mother, and sittings were arranged for Miss Lindner at Buckingham Palace, and the Royal Mews at Windsor.

The Queen Mother later gave the Worcester Royal Porcelain Company permission to make a hundred numbered copies, chiefly for export. The price when issued was one hundred and fifty guineas each and these models seldom change hands today, but one came up for auction a few years ago, and it may be of interest to note that it fetched nearly £6,000 at a London auction.

In 1967 Doris Lindner made an equestrian porcelain portrait of His Royal Highness the Duke of Edinburgh on his polo pony 'Inez', which makes a pair with the earlier portrait model of the Queen, although of course that of the Duke portrays a less formal occasion. Later she also modelled Princess Anne on 'Doublet'.

Each model takes approximately twelve months to go through the various processes from the time Miss Lindner makes the first impression of her subject. Her colours are always lifelike, the porcelain of the finest quality and the workmanship comparable to that of the famous original Continental master-potters.

4. *Doris Lindner's famous equestrian portrait of the Queen when, as Princess Elizabeth, she took the salute on the horse 'Tommy' on behalf of her father, King George VI, at the 1947 Trooping of the Colour*

5. *Doris Lindner's much sought after models of the Horse Guards and Life Guards, now the Blues and Royals*

Comparisons with priceless early Worcester pieces can be made at the Dyson Perrins Museum, and it will be seen that in the hands of fine artists like Dorothy Doughty and Doris Lindner, porcelain can be a magnificent medium for sculpture. In the years to come their work will undoubtedly rank among the fine art treasures of the twentieth century.

Modelling in fine porcelain appeals to many talented artists on both sides of the Atlantic, most of whom specialise in one particular subject. Ronald van Ruyckevelt, however, who is one of the world's great porcelain sculptors, is unusually versatile and models Royal Queens and fashionable Victorian ladies with the same skill as tropical fish and marine plants, game birds and garden flowers and blossoms.

He has travelled the world in the course of his work, and spent some years designing and modelling for Royal Worcester Porcelain Company in Britain, but in 1973 he relocated to Monterey, California, with his family, where he has estab-

6. *Mr and Mrs Ronald van Ruyckevelt in their studio at Monterey, California*

lished his own studio and continues to produce fine work –
true collectors' pieces.

Royal Worcester continue to issue some models of his exquisite work such as the recent series of Queens Regnant. The first
two figures in this series are Mary I (1553–1558) and Elizabeth I
(1558–1603), both models limited to an edition of 250. They
are superb portraits with authentic detail taken from historic
paintings. This series will include Mary II (1689–1694), Anne
(1702–1714), Victoria (1837–1901), and H.M. Queen
Elizabeth II – which is to be released during 1977, the Jubilee
year of her reign.

Although it is impossible to mention the many skilled
ceramic sculptors working today, those discussed in this chapter are timeless in their appeal and their work can certainly be
counted among antiques for the future.

7. 'Susannah' from Ronald van Ruyckevelt's American Heritage Series,
exquisite sculptures of 19th-century American women. The original of the
hatbox can be seen at Claverton Manor, Bath, The American Museum in
Britain

# 3  EMBROIDERY MAKES HISTORY IN THE 1970s

Needlework and embroidery have always appealed to collectors, and examples which have been casually handed down from one generation to another can form the basis of a fine collection and start one on the fascinating and rewarding study of stitches, fabrics, origins of patterns and designs which this involves.

In Britain a flourishing tradition of domestic needlework has existed from the sixteenth century onwards, but during the last twenty-five years there has been a startling renaissance of interest in embroidery and stitchery of all kinds, the study of which now has an important place in Colleges of Art. It is no longer seen as an isolated subject, but knowledge of drawing, painting, sculpture, design and even architecture contribute to needlework in the modern idiom. The influence of these subjects as well as the wide variety of stitches with their special functions lead to some interesting three-dimensional effects. This is specially true of stitchery combined with collage, using different fabrics and textures, almost as an artist uses paint from his palate.

Needlework has thereby been promoted from an elegant pastime to a vital art form with new uses and effects characteristic of our times. Present-day examples will undoubtedly go forward into history like those which have come down to us from former times.

It is possible to acquire potentially valuable examples of the best of today's skilled stitchery, as there are a number of exhibitions organised by art schools and colleges where the work of advanced students of needlework is shown. For example, the Royal School of Needlework in London and the Embroidery Guild both exhibit their students' work from time to time. The Women's Institute also hold an annual show in London which includes some examples of highly skilled needlework and other important exhibitions are organised in various parts of the country.

The choice for today's collector is therefore wide, but it is really worth while to specialise in a particular field that appeals to you. Unfortunately, although needlework has once more become recognised as an art, few embroiderers sign their work, and therefore their names are not known in the art world in the same way as those of painters, sculptors and many other craftsmen. It would be a good plan for a collector when buying an individual piece of contemporary embroidery to ask the artist concerned to stitch his or her signature thereon, as this would certainly add to the interest of the various pieces as the years go by.

Embroidery is no longer just a popular recreation among ladies of leisure, but is returning to the hands of professional artist-craftsmen and women, who are commissioned to carry out large projects, as in the thirteenth and fourteenth centuries, when a style of needlework now known as 'Opus Anglicanum' was produced in London workshops. This work was in demand all over Europe and is still treasured in many cathedrals and museums.

For centuries the Christian Church has been an important patron and user of embroidery, and indeed has depended upon it as one of the decorative arts, together with stained glass, carving and sculpture, to communicate the mysteries of many Bible truths. Artists have long used their talents in churches and cathedrals to the glory of God, and before literacy was general, many members of the congregation learned Bible stories about God and the Saints from pictorial representations. Ecclesiastical vestments, altar frontals and other church furnishings, are among the fabulous pieces of needlework handed down to us from the past.

After World War II, when many churches and cathedrals had suffered bomb damage, a vital opportunity occurred for competent church embroiderers to renew and restore this loss. Beryl Dean, M.B.E., who is one of the best-known British professionals in this field, saw the opportunity and turned her talents in this direction. Her superb work is now in many cathedrals and churches in England, America and other parts of the world, and she has many important commissions in hand. She tells me she began training at the Royal School of Needlework, but longed from the beginning to do design. At that time Rebecca Crompton had been on the staff at Croydon School of Art and was a very great influence on the teaching of embroidery. Beryl Dean studied in the 1930s with one of this artist's famous pupils, Elizabeth Thomson, when the modern idiom in embroidery really began, and she was awarded a Royal Exhibition, enabling her to go to the Royal College of Art, where she had a wide art training and specialised in Dress Designing. She also lectured at Durham University and elsewhere on various allied subjects. Her great desire was to do her own work, so she gave up full-time teaching and combined this with a part-time post at the Stanhope Institute of Education.

Twenty years ago she first felt that ecclesiastical embroidery was a neglected subject and that the whole field required fresh thought, so she began to specialise. Firstly she realised that people needed to see a modern approach in church needlework, so she did what she could to bring to it those new ideas already apparent in contemporary secular embroidery; she attempted to get more interest into the design and colour of ecclesiastical needlework, and not to be limited by tradition. Her previous wide training was invaluable in this.

The next thing she realised was that clear instructions in teaching and lecturing were not enough to nurture the seeds of this new approach, and so she wrote her first book *Ecclesiastical Embroidery*, now in its fourth edition. By this time the fresh thinking on the subject was beginning to influence

1. *and* 2. *Examples of work designed and embroidered by Beryl Dean. Left, St Catherine, purchased for the Church of St James the Less in Mount Eliza, Victoria, Australia. Above, 'The Visit of the Magi', the third of five panels for the Rutland Chantry, St George's Chapel, Windsor*

schools of art and she herself was teaching at Hammersmith College of Art where was established the first course in Ecclesiastical Embroidery.

Beryl Dean's work has been exhibited in America and Australia, where several important pieces are now permanently in use. One of her most recent commissions in Britain (1968) was for five panels for the Rutland Chantry of St George's Chapel, Windsor, designed by herself. She was given seven New Testament subjects from which to select the themes for these panels which were to replace hangings that were old and faded, and she chose the Annunciation, the Visitation, the Nativity, the Temptation and the Marriage at Cana. These panels were completed in 1974 and before being moved to Windsor were exhibited in St Andrew's Church, Holborn – along with a magnificent collection of her work and that of her students.

Her present activities include teaching and lecturing (at the Stanhope Institute and elsewhere) and the carrying out of important commissions, both here and in America. One of these is a magnificent cope for the new Archbishop of Canterbury.

Two historically important pieces of commissioned needlework of an entirely different kind have been produced in recent years by The Royal School of Needlework. They are somewhat reminiscent of the Bayeux Tapestries but depicting history in the idiom of today, making use of such modern techniques as appliqué and collage, or what is now called in America 'assemblage'. These important pieces of work are the historic Hastings Embroideries and the 'Overlord Embroidery' commissioned by Lord Dulverton. The latter, designed by Sandra Lawrence, comprises thirty-four panels graphically depicting the invasion of Normandy in 1944. These panels are said to be the largest work of their kind in the world, and were carried out at The Royal School of Needlework, as were the Hastings Embroideries of 1966 commemorating the nine hundredth anniversary of the Battle of Hastings. These con-

3. *Royal School of Needlework students working on the Hastings Embroidery*

sist of twenty-seven separately framed panels, nine feet long by three feet – a total length of 243 feet.

The eighty-one panels portray important events in British history and are worked in a mixture of appliqué and threads, cords, metals and stitchery. The pictures that guided the designing artists were obtained from royal palaces, the Houses of Parliament, museums and books and the panels were drawn symbolically. The panels were then embroidered in the high tradition of the Royal School of Needlework and form a unique work of art. This fine school, established in London in 1872, aims to 'restore ornamental needlework for secular purposes to the high place it once held among the decorative arts'.

4. Above, *panel one of the Hastings Embroidery commissioned to celebrate the 900th anniversary of the Battle of Hastings*

5. Below, *panel six of the Hastings Embroidery, 'The Beginning of our Parliament'*

6. *A ten-foot altar frontal by Margaret Kaye which was purchased by the Queen and presented to Accra Cathedral*

During the hundred years of its existence it has maintained a high standard of craftsmanship both as a teaching school and workshop. In 1906, feeling that not enough attention was being given to actual embroidery design, sixteen past students of the Royal School of Needlework founded The Embroiderers' Guild 'to promote the design and art functions of Embroidery'. It now has a large teaching structure in London, and forty-two country branches with twenty-eight overseas affiliated societies.

Much contemporary embroidery, however, relies on commercial designs or classical patterns and work that is based on original designs is rare, and therefore all the more precious.

The work of Margaret Kaye, for example, comes in this category. She was one of the earliest artists of this period to find her special medium in fabric collage, combined with stitchery. She studied stained glass at Croydon School of Art and The Royal College of Art, and has carried out important commissions for stained glass windows, altar frontals, etc. The rich colouring she uses in her needlework and the broad effects show the influence of her studies of stained glass. This

artist has held a number of one-man shows at the Roland Browse & Delbanco Galleries in London, and has executed commissions for ecclesiastical authorities and shipping lines at home and abroad.

Her work has been purchased by some leading museums, including the Victoria and Albert, and is in many private collections.

Another artist of outstanding merit in vivid fabric collages is Vera Sherman who, for the past ten years, has also organised travelling exhibitions entitled 'Contemporary Hangings', which have brought to public notice work of outstanding merit in this dramatic decorative medium now in fashion.

The tapestry wall hangings of past centuries have been complemented today by the work of many outstanding artists too numerous to mention here. Vera Sherman's excellent book, *Wall Hangings of Today*, will introduce the reader to the varied and original work of over thirty of them, many of whom already have work in public and private collections where it expresses the vital talents of the seventies and awaits its turn to become the next century's antiques.

# 4 TODAY'S FABULOUS ENGRAVED GLASS

Glass, one of the oldest and most magical man-made substances, has always been collectable and has never been finer than it is today. We take its many forms for granted in everyday use, but there is nothing in the world quite like it.

It appears in nature as rock crystal, a form of quartz which for centuries past has been carved and engraved by craftsmen to make precious and beautiful objects. Also a volcanic rock, obsidian, found in many parts of the world resembles a black, brown or greenish bottle glass. This is formed by the rapid cooling of volcanic lava, the hard fragments of which break leaving sharp curved edges, and these were used by primitive man to make weapons and such things as knives, scrapers and arrow-heads.

Pliny included a story in his writings about a party of Phoenician sailor merchants, who went ashore and camped on a sandy beach by the mouth of a river in Syria. To make a fire they used some cargo from their ship, that contained a small quantity of carbonate of soda and some rocks. Next morning, when the camp fire had cooled, it is said they found beneath the ashes that the sand and soda had fused together into a kind of glass.

Whether this was truly the first instance of man-made glass it is hard to tell, but it is highly probable that it was discovered by a lucky accident such as this, and it appears that the Syrians and Egyptians were the first great glass-makers. Their work can still be seen in museums as can that of the Romans who, learning from them, also became highly skilled in this art.

A famous glass industry settled near Venice, from where

the rudimentary principles of glass-making spread over Europe, and were developed as man's demands became more sophisticated. It was realised that by taking some ordinary natural materials such as sand, soda, lime, lead and the ashes of various trees and plants, versatile and useful transparent substances could be produced which lent themselves to great artistry in both decoration and usage.

Antique glass needs no introduction to present-day collectors. Its beauty, elegance and variety have fascinated connoisseurs for centuries, and in spite of its delicacy, much of it has miraculously survived the years.

Today many fine artists are working in this medium whose talents and accomplishments are undoubtedly producing masterpieces that will become valuable antiques in the future. For example, there are some specially fine glass engravers. This form of decoration was used with great delicacy after 1745 when an excise tax was imposed on glass, based on weight. George Ravenscroft's glass of lead, with its brilliant texture and wonderful properties for retaining and dispersing light was one of the most important developments in English crystal glass during the seventeenth century, but it lent itself to the heavy and elaborate decoration in vogue at the time, and was no longer practicable after the tax.

The glass-makers, faced with this tax, turned their talents to delicate engraving on thinner glass, first with a diamond point, and later with the cutter's wheel; all of course had to be worked by hand. The engraver's point had been used on glass in different ways from classical times, the design being scratched out in line and the tone provided by cross-hatching or stippling. Dutch engravers excelled in this work which also spread to England and elsewhere in Europe. The engravers sat at a revolving lathe using a variety of little copper discs. It was a most delicate process and required great skill. Some of the earliest of this hand-wheel engraving took the form of heraldic designs, but later English engravers turned to the more characteristic floral and naturalistic patterns at about the same period as the Staffordshire potters were depicting roses and garden flowers and foliage in great profusion on porcelain. Contemporary events and sporting scenes were also skilfully hand-engraved on glass in the eighteenth century. By 1760 hand-cut crystal glass returned to favour and it continued to increase in popularity during the following 150 years or so. The Victorians used elaborately and rather heavily cut glass in profusion, bearing handsome designs appropriate to their elaborate furnishings.

Today cut crystal glass has reached a very high standard indeed in the hands of a number of traditional British manufacturers and it is exported all over the world. Famous glass-makers in the United States of America and on the continent of Europe are also creating masterpieces in this wonderful man-made substance, but perhaps the most characteristic of today's glass treasures are those decorated by some fine individual engravers, whose accomplishments in this field are of exceptional quality, and will surely be treasured for generations to come.

The work of Laurence Whistler now deservedly fetches fabulous sums on the rare occasions when it comes up for auction. For example the goblet made by Whitefriars Glass and engraved by Laurence Whistler in 1965 (see illustration opposite), was recently sold at Christie's for close on a thousand pounds.

Laurence Whistler was born in 1912, educated at Balliol College, Oxford, and was the younger brother of Rex Whistler, the artist. He is a self-taught engraver, and having started life as a poet and writer, with a number of books published, he began engraving glass in 1935. He works now mostly on blown glass, designing his own shapes and he also designs and works on church windows and window panes in private houses. He has held several one-man exhibitions in Britain, and joined in group exhibitions at the Festival Hall, London in 1962 and the Corning Museum of Glass, New York, in 1974. Many of his fine pieces of work are now on permanent exhibi-

1. *A goblet engraved by Laurence Whistler and depicting summer and winter. Christie's of London sold it recently for 950 guineas*

tion in public galleries and museums in Britain and the USA.

John Hutton from New Zealand carried out a very important piece of engraved glass for a screen in Coventry Cathedral when it was re-built after the blitz of World War II. He designed and engraved a number of life-sized angels in the modern idiom, a truly monumental piece of work which will doubtless be admired by many generations to come – one of the many contemporary treasures in this twentieth-century cathedral.

Another exceptionally fine glass engraver and designer is Peter Dreiser, who now chiefly undertakes private commissions of a very high standard. He was born in 1936, and from 1951–54 studied at the Technical Glass School, Rheinbach, Bonn, and specialised in wheel-engraving (copper, stone and diamond). In 1955 he made his home in England, and became a member of the Society of Designer Craftsmen and of the Crafts Centre of Great Britain. He worked in industry for

2. and 3. Work by Peter Dreiser. Right, *an Orrefors decanter 'Standing on the fall'*. Below, *an Orrefors bowl engraved using the copper wheel method*

some years and then joined Thomas Goode and Company of South Audley Street, London, where he stayed for eight years, during which time he was responsible for some important commissions such as engraved commemorative goblets, bowls, and other fine personalised presentation pieces for state occasions.

In 1970 he became a freelance craftsman with his own workshop meeting the growing demand for his engraved glass and also enjoying the freedom to experiment with abstract designs and varied techniques, in all of which he displays the same superb skill. Unlike many glass artists he signs his many fine pieces of work.

I asked Peter Dreiser why he decided to make England his home when the Continent has such excellent facilities for glass-workers of all kinds, including glass colleges. He said that the general renaissance in Britain of all the crafts, and the consequent appreciation and demand for the finest work of contemporary artist-craftsmen provides an encouraging atmosphere for individual creative work that he finds especially congenial. An important development that has recently taken place in this connection is the formation of the Guild of Glass Engravers of which he is a member of the Working Committee. This guild was formed in 1975 and is presided over by Laurence Whistler. It now has some hundred enthusiastic members and is growing steadily.

Most of the glass engravers in Britain are of necessity self-taught as, with the exception of tuition in glass-cutting and engraving in Edinburgh, few art schools at present have the necessary facilities, although it seems that there is a great demand for the subject. Peter Dreiser himself teaches glass engraving to a class of enthusiastic students at Morley College one evening a week, but he would like to see more facilities for tuition with modern equipment in glass art developing in art schools and colleges along the lines of the other fine crafts, such as silversmithing and pottery. In spite of so little organised tuition, glass engravers in this country with their versatile talents and enthusiasm, excel in this beautiful art form, and many pieces of their work will no doubt be valued for generations to come when they are 'antiques of the future'.

Several of the British glass manufacturers in Stourbridge and in Scotland have specialised in using the work of some very accomplished glass engravers on their superb quality glassware. (See the illustration opposite of an example of the work of Michael Fairbairn on Stuart Crystal.) Two hundred of these pieces form part of a series produced in collaboration with the World Wildlife Fund, which will consist of pieces of engraved crystal showing some fifty species of wildlife that are liable to become extinct. Michael Fairbairn also produced a twelve-inch plate on Stuart Crystal entitled 'The Partridge'. This was commissioned by the Game Conservancy and presented to their President, Prince Philip, Duke of Edinburgh. These splendid pieces of engraved glass are definitely in the heirloom class.

Perhaps more within the reach of the average collector, Strathearn Glass of Crieff, Scotland, have produced a recent series of glass vases engraved by their accomplished artist, Alasdair C. Gordon. In this series, various methods of engraving are used such as stone wheel, diamond burr, copper wheel and sand blast. Although the engraving is all hand work and individually designed, modern drills, wheels, etc. which are powered by electricity, give the artist greater freedom while on this delicate work. The BBC recently commissioned a glass bowl, engraved by Alasdair C. Gordon to be presented as the trophy for 'Mastermind'.

Whatever the method of glass engraving, it is always a delicate operation. The age-old technique of diamond point engraving is still practised, and designs and scrolls of great delicacy can be achieved. In recent years, however, the use of dental cutting tools, inserted into high speed pneumatic grinders, has created new possibilities for the craftsman, and several different methods can now be used on the same piece of work, enabling the artist-designer to obtain a wider variety of

4. *A hand-engraved motif of a Giant Panda by Michael Fairbairn*

effects; for example, sand blasting, which is a twentieth-century method of creating designs on glass, both intaglio and in shallow relief. This method cannot, however, compete with fine copper wheel engraving for subtlety of modelling and fine, sensitive detail, in both of which the finest twentieth-century glass engravers excel – their individual creations doubtless to become valuable antiques in the future.

5. *Strathearn engraved crystal glass with heron design*

# 5 STUDIO POTTERY OF THE TWENTIETH CENTURY IS COLLECTABLE

This century has seen a great expansion and development in the work of studio potters in Europe and elsewhere.

Perhaps the present widespread demand for this work has been produced by a revulsion from mass-produced articles and the desire of many people to possess a genuine original work of art, however small; after all, even a hand-made mug can have its own very special character and charm.

Whatever the cause, there is now a very real appreciation of the potters' art and much of their work is of a high standard of design and workmanship. It is also, usually, moderate in price, so the average collector can avail him or herself of the opportunity to acquire some excellent pieces, which will surely be looked upon by future generations as antiques of the twentieth century.

The influence of Bernard Leach since about 1911 has undoubtedly been responsible for the foundation for much of this development. His innate sense of beauty, his idealism and a depth of feeling that goes far beyond mere technique, together with a high sense of spiritual values and a real capacity for hard work, have produced a vitality which has had far-reaching effects on the craft of studio pottery, and even on those many other crafts which now hold such an important place in the art world.

Bernard Leach was born in Hong Kong in 1887, but was educated in England at Beaumont College. When he was sixteen years of age he went to the Slade School of Art and studied drawing under Henry Tonks. He also studied at the London School of Art. At twenty-one, attracted by the writ-

1. *A fluted bowl in porcelain by Bernard Leach, included in the Travelling Exhibition for Europe for British Potters, arranged by the Crafts Advisory Committee in association with the British Council*

ings of Lafcadio Hearn, he went to Japan and studied under a representative of the sixth generation of Kenzans.* He lived and studied in Japan for eleven years, making some visits to Peking, but returned to England in 1920. His work was then unique in the field of modern ceramics, as he was the first Westerner to have studied oriental pottery techniques and to work in the oriental idiom. Leach returned to England with Shoji Hamada and, working together, they were undoubtedly the forerunners of the contemporary pottery movement in the West today.

On his return to Britain Leach set up the Leach Pottery at St Ives and with his hand-built traditional kiln began making Raku and Stoneware, which he had studied in the East, but he soon included slip decorated lead-glazed earthenware. He also took on some good students who eventually became well-known themselves in their own right, so that student

---

*A Japanese family famous for their Raku pottery, calligraphy and painting. Leach studied under the last of this remarkable family.

*2. A stoneware bottle in black and rust by Bernard Leach*

apprentices were attracted to the pottery from all over the world. At the same time there was a steadily increasing demand for good hand-made tableware.

In 1966 Bernard Leach received the Japanese Order of the Sacred Treasure, Second Class, which is the highest honour given to a British commoner. He has written several books and received many important awards, including the CBE and the Binns Medal of the American Ceramics Society and has had over 100 worldwide exhibitions, both one-man and in groups of work by other important artist-craftsmen. He still lectures and demonstrates in many countries, having travelled extensively in all parts of the world, and the relationship that he established between the potters of Britain and of Japan is of great significance in the history of modern ceramics. The possession of a piece of his work would be of great importance to any collector.

Another exceptional potter of our time is Lucie Rie, and it is said that she was the first female studio potter to gain a high reputation. She was born in Australia in 1902, trained in Vienna and had gained a considerable reputation and many awards on the Continent before settling in England in 1938, where she met Bernard Leach, and watching him at work made a deep impression on her. Although her pots are not directly influenced by him, their friendship has greatly helped her to develop work of great individuality.

In 1939 she established a workshop in London's Albion Mews, a converted garage, but during the war years she had to give up her pottery to work in a factory. In 1946 Hans Coper joined her and she began to rediscover her own style of work but as yet there was little appreciation for her pots. In 1950 her first exhibitions were held in London and Dartington. A show at Bonniers in New York was followed by a mass of orders and her work began to be appreciated by a discriminating public. Her stature as a potter has become widely recognised in Britain and abroad, and in 1967 the Arts Council held a retrospective exhibition of her work – a rare honour. Bernard Leach has said: 'An outstanding quality of Lucie Rie's work is the degree to which it is free from the direct influence of other potters, ancient and modern. . . . She has the rare faculty of digesting influences by passing them through the mesh of her own character.'

Hans Coper, who worked with her from 1946–58, came to England from Germany in 1939, and although he had been trained as an engineer, he had also studied painting and sculpture. When he went to assist Lucie Rie in her London studio, he found his vocation to be in this medium, and later established his own pottery in Somerset. He has his own individual style, using a Continental-type wheel, foot-operated, and enjoys the sensitive control which this gives in throwing. All his pots are thrown and each one is intensely individual, even though this dedicated craftsman returns again and again to a few basic shapes.

3. *A flattened bottle in oxidised stoneware by Lucie Rie, first shown at the British Craft Centre and included in the Travelling Exhibition for Europe*

4. *A small bottle with a flat top in oxidised stoneware with burnished manganese engobe by Hans Coper, first shown at the British Craft Centre and included in the Travelling Exhibition for Europe*

Michael Casson is another studio potter whose work is now sought after. Amongst other places in London it is available at Liberty's in their new 'One Off' department which consists of commissioned pieces by a variety of today's best craftsmen in all their different fields. Here many collectors' pieces in pot-

5. *Stoneware vases or large jars (two feet high) made by Michael Casson*

tery, silver, woodware and bronze, are exhibited and are for
sale. Collectors in London also flock to the British Craft
Centre at 43 Earlham Street, WC2, the Craft Shop at the
Victoria and Albert Museum, the Craftsmen Potters' Shop in
William Blake's House, Marshall Street, and the craft shop in
the Design Centre in the Haymarket. In all these places they
will find a good selection of studio pottery. Most other towns
also now have souvenir shops where pieces of hand-made
pottery are for sale and though naturally some of these pieces
are of better quality and design than others, much of the work
expresses the spirit of this century, and if you choose something that really appeals to you, it may well take its own place
in your collection as an antique of the future.

One interesting indication of this is that studio pottery has
recently been included in important sales at Christie's and
Sotheby's, together with pieces of Art Nouveau and other
good twentieth-century ceramics, and the demand for really
fine pieces is rising.

The formation of the British Craft Centre at 12 Waterloo
Place, W1, has accomplished much and continues to publicise
the work of many fine artist-craftsmen in this country. The
travelling exhibitions organised by this organisation and their
index of established craftsmen are helpful to the public and
also to the many fine craftsmen who are too busy with their art
to publicise their own work, much of which is carried out in
remote parts of the countryside. This central point of contact
in London fulfils a long-felt need.

In a field where today's fine craftsmen are still charging
reasonable prices for their work, a wise and selective buyer
may well purchase an heirloom for the future.

# PART 2   TREASURES OF YESTERDAY AND TODAY

# 6 DIAMONDS ARE FOR EVER

Much of the jewellery made before the nineteenth century is only known to us as displayed in museums or in important private collections. It cannot therefore be handled or seen worn in the way it was intended, so its beauty and charm cannot be fully appreciated.

Luckily, however, the Victorians loved jewellery and wore a quantity of it and much of this has survived. Indeed, during the last decade Victorian jewellery has become the vogue, both among collectors and also as a fashionable adornment, and is now looked upon as 'antique'.

Unfortunately during the time, not long past, when Victoriana of all kinds was not sought after, much of the jewellery of the period was broken up, the gold melted down and the gem-stones re-cut and reset in more 'up to date' designs.

It is cause for satisfaction, however, that the craftsmen-jewellers of the nineteenth century used a wide variety of materials in addition to precious stones, gold and silver, so that much of their work did not tempt the breaker-up and it is still possible for a discerning collector to find a selection of interesting pieces, although no longer at the bargain prices of a few years ago. Gone are the days when Victorian jewellery could be picked up for the proverbial 'song', in junk shops, 'back street' jewellers or pawnbrokers.

Interesting pieces of Victorian workmanship have now been promoted to shop windows where high quality goods are displayed, and anyone who is fortunate enough to find Granny's muff chain or Auntie's cameo brooch when spring-cleaning the attic, is today the lucky possessor of a veritable

1. and 2. Above, *two Victorian love rings. The first letters of each stone make up a word.* Right, *ruby, emerald, garnet, amethyst, ruby, diamond for 'regard'.* Left, *diamond, emerald, amethyst, ruby, emerald, sapphire, topas for 'dearest'.* Below, *a set of brooch and earrings made with textured gold by Gerald Benny*

treasure. We wonder what present-day jewellery will be looked upon as desirable antiques in a hundred years from now? It is hard to say – the choice is wide, but somewhat perplexing.

Able young jewellers abound. Mostly their work is in precious metals which has an intrinsic value quite apart from the workmanship. Will this fine work suffer the heart-breaking fate of being melted down like many Victorian pieces, as taste and fashion change? We trust not, but the public is fickle in its demands.

A specially intriguing trend in much of today's jewellery is the inclusion of chunky, natural mineral substances. These stones are not considered gems and are set in such pieces as rings, pendants and necklaces, uncut and unpolished, in all their natural beauty. They are decorative and colourful and it seems almost magical that they lay in the rock formations of the earth for thousands and sometimes millions of years. The recent craze for 'rock hunting' has brought their beauty to light and opened to others what was once the province of geologists and scientists. This rugged fashion may well fascinate future generations and be recognisable as of 'mid to late twentieth-century workmanship'.

Textured gold and silver is another characteristic of present-day jewellery, taking its inspiration from nature, the bark of trees or ripples on water, and so on. Design of all kinds always keeps pace with other visual arts so modern jewellery and silver-smithing will be seen to echo the spirit of contemporary architecture, sculpture, painting, embroidery, and other art forms.

There is a great deal of encouragement for today's young craftsmen jewellers. For example, the Worshipful Company of Goldsmiths in the City of London sponsor various competitions and hold frequent exhibitions of contemporary work at Goldsmith's Hall, Foster Lane, London, EC2, and much of this work is of a very high standard. For decades the Company has been Britain's – and possibly the world's – leading patron of modern silver and jewellery. During this period the number of British designers working in these mediums has greatly increased. This startling growth can best be seen in the numbers of pieces of gold and silver hallmarked in the Assay Office at Goldsmiths' Hall which has reached into millions. For example they state that they tested and marked no less than 7,692,563 pieces in 1974. Their Crafts Committee's policy has also done much to encourage public appreciation of fine work in precious metals and to find and help producers of excellent design and craftsmanship by exhibiting, publicising and buying their work. Many of these pieces have also been exhibited abroad. One of the first exhibitions of modern jewellery in the world was shown at Goldsmith's Hall in the City of London in 1961, and British jewellery has been said to set the pace in creative craftsmanship ever since.

The Worshipful Company of Goldsmiths also took a new initiative recently in organising an exhibition at Goldsmiths' Hall entitled 'Loot' in which everything was for sale (an entirely new departure) and, on this occasion, everything shown was priced at under £50, to demonstrate that fine workmanship and interesting pieces of jewellery need not be impossibly expensive. They certainly achieved their object, as many of the pieces exhibited were of a high standard of workmanship and modern design and were made from an interesting and wide variety of materials.

It was stated in the catalogue of the exhibition that 'Loot' was 'aimed at the huge day-time population of the City of London who use typewriters more than tiaras' and the Company 'believe that British craftsmen have risen to the occasion to prove that one can buy well for a modest price'. Several pieces of work from the actual exhibition and other pieces by some of the exhibitors are illustrated in this book.

De Beers Consolidated Mines, the famous diamond merchants, also contribute a great deal to the sponsorship and patronage of jewellery today. For example, they sponsor the 'Diamonds International Awards' and 'Diamonds Today'

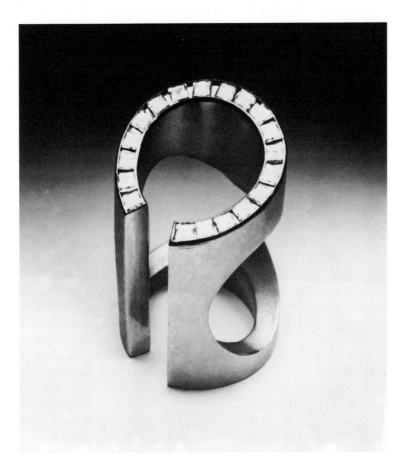

3. *Professor Hiramatsu of Japan designed this unusual platinum ring which is set with nineteen square-cut diamonds. It was presented to the winning jockey of a King George VI and the Queen Elizabeth Diamond Stakes race at Ascot*

competitions to encourage excellence in modern jewellery design. They also do everything possible to assist students to use diamonds in the best and most exciting ways, realising that these students are the jewellers of the future. In addition to this they sponsor the biggest horserace in the British Horse Racing Calendar, 'The King George VI and the Queen Elizabeth Diamond Stakes' and commission designers from all over the world to make trophies and jewellery for this race.

4. *One of the winning designs from 1303 entries in the 1973 Diamonds International Awards. It is by Ernest Blyth*

5. *Another winner in the 1973 competition in a very contrasting style by Barbara Tipple*

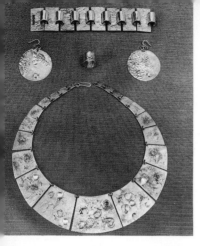

6. *and* 7. Left, *work by John Grenville representing the surface of the* *moon.* Right, *ancient stone beads re-used by Lady Dale in a modern style*

A number of leading jewellers also encourage young craftsmen and women by employing consultant designers on their staff and many hold exhibitions on their premises. For example, Cameo Corner, the famous antique jewellers in Museum Street, London, usually hold an exhibition – which often includes modern jewellery – before Christmas each year. Last year it was called 'Jewels '75'. Some work included in one of their recent summer exhibitions, 'Gem Engravings' by Ronald Pennell, is illustrated opposite.

Nearly twenty years ago gem engraving was said to be a lost art in Britain. Complex techniques, with each type of stone requiring a different treatment, had to be developed, often by trial and error. Ronald Pennell, one of the most skilled workers in this field, studied in Britain and on the Continent, and has exhibited his work widely. He finds inspiration in unusual subjects and achieves a feeling of spontanaeity and subtle humour in his engravings, despite the hours of intricate and often tedious work involved in the high standard of craftsmanship. The engravings are carved in intaglio, mostly in crystal or citrine, on the reverse side, to be viewed from the front of the stone, giving an unusual three-dimensional effect. Every one of Pennell's gems is unique and bears his entwined initials as signature. Whether mounted in gold or silver as brooches, rings or pendants, lids of boxes, or just as engraved gems, each one is a collectors' piece, and without doubt will become an antique of the future.

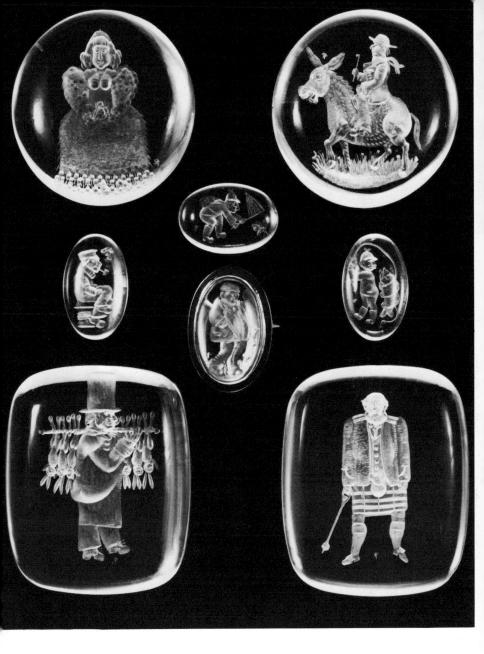

8. *Examples of Ronald Pennell's unique style of gem engraving in the modern idiom*

9. *A silver hamlet by Michael Burton shown at a recent 'Loot' exhibition in London's Goldsmiths' Hall*

Some work by Jocelyn Burton, see the illustration on page 122, was shown at the 'Loot' exhibition, and she is certainly one of the many accomplished contemporary British woman jewellers and silversmiths. She uses natural form with a modern interpretation for many of her designs, feeling that the present era is one when originality of design has full scope and freedom to affect the taste and change the attitude of the general public. It is one of her cherished ambitions to contribute to this change.

She was recently commissioned by the Worshipful Company of Goldsmiths to design the hallmark for platinum and this is now being used. Her brother, Michael Burton, also exhibited at 'Loot'. He is inspired by the countryside in his work and specialises in carving and chasing silver country cottages. One of his silver hamlets, which seems to unite the old with the new, is illustrated opposite.

The talented young craftsmen working today are too numerous to mention in the space at our disposal and we have had to pick out just a few to represent the modern trends.

It is interesting that Edwardian jewellery seems insignificant to the present generation, but perhaps the very delicacy of the small stones in dainty settings that were used early in this century will appeal to collectors a few years from now, before the impact of today's striking pieces overtakes them. For the tranquillity of the Edwardian era with its delicacy of sentiment expressed in gifts of jewellery and trinkets has been overshadowed by a veritable explosion in the modern crafts – an explosion which will surely mark the present period an important one for future collectors.

Jewellery is one of the oldest of the decorative arts and precious stones have answered a deep human love of beauty through the ages. The romance of gems created and formed by nature, lying deep under the earth's surface for thousands of years, is magic in itself and it is a profound thought that the first diamonds are believed to have been discovered around 600 BC and are everlasting. No doubt many ancient diamonds are still in use, re-cut and set to suit the art of subsequent generations. Their wonderful sparkle will continue for generations to come.

# 7  COMMEMORATIVES CAN BE FUN

The field of commemoratives in Britain alone is so vast that collectors of widely different tastes and means can find something to appeal to them at a price they can afford.

For the beginner collector it is as well to decide in the first place what is a commemorative?

The strict view is that it is an object that records a particular event, and it will usually bear an inscription and date identifying it with that event. Royal occasions, political or historic happenings such as wars or individual battles and important discoveries, such as man's landing on the moon are subjects of commemorative art.

Henry Sandon, the well-known writer and authority on ceramics, takes the view that to be considered as a genuine commemorative an object must, to a certain extent, be mass-produced, with every piece virtually the same; he therefore considers that the production in 1757 of transfer printed mugs and other pieces to commemorate the King of Prussia, marked the true beginning at Worcester of the making of commemoratives which flourished until the end of the nineteenth century.

Anniversary pieces form a category of their own, as do stamps, medals and valuable silverware, but ceramic pieces are perhaps the most plentiful and cover such a variety of subjects and in so many different forms that they are the most readily available to the average collector who must specialise according to his own taste and circumstances.

Royal commemoratives have become prolific since the early nineteenth century and are now widely collected. The oldest known examples are some now rare English Delft pieces made to record the Restoration of Charles II. One of these, an English Delft wine cup dated 1660 and decorated with a portrait of Charles II, was sold at Christie's in February 1975 for 2700 guineas. At the time of writing this is believed to be a record sum for such an item to date.

Larger numbers of ceramic commemoratives began to be produced in 1761 with those printed to celebrate the wedding and coronation of King George III and Queen Charlotte. These were made in porcelain and in pottery and pieces depicting these events are known to have been made in Worcester, Longton Hall, Derby, and Bow porcelain, also in a series of Wedgwood cream-ware tea pots.

Actually Wedgwood, one of the most prolific British pottery factories, have been making a good selection of commemorative items for eighty years or more, and continue to do so. Wedgwood's Queens Ware did not lend itself to commemorative items, but their Basalt and Jasper did, and is used a great deal for this purpose today.

For example, Jasper medallions were ideal for commemorating events of national and international importance, but early examples of these made during the reign of George III have now become rare, and are looked upon as museum pieces. With the accession to the throne of Queen Victoria, the era of commemorative pottery really began throughout the industry; until towards the end of her reign almost every event from the China Wars to her Diamond Jubilee found expression in commemorative pots.

Wedgwood excelled in these, and continue to this day to record important events of present-day history, such as the Queen's coronation and silver wedding or the first moon landing, with mugs, sweet dishes, ash trays and bonbonnieres. Important historical and sporting events like the bi-centenary of the Declaration of Independence and the Olympic Games are also recorded.

Royal Doulton, Spode and The Worcester Royal Porcelain

1. *and* 2. *Commemorative items from the coronation of Queen Elizabeth II in 1953.* Above *from Wedgwood and Sons Ltd, and* below *designs by Agnette Hoy from Doulton and Co. Ltd*

Company have also issued quantities of interesting commemoratives during the last 150 years, and continue to do so now.

The *Illustrated London News* of 25 June 1887 published an account of how the Doulton beaker was distributed to thirty thousand London schoolchildren in Hyde Park as part of Queen Victoria's Jubilee festivities. Refreshments, such as buns and milk, were provided for these children, and each one

3. *A collector's piece from Wedgwood commemorating man's first landing on the moon*

was also presented with a jubilee memorial mug of which
45,000 were manufactured by Messrs. Doulton and Company
at the Burslem Pottery, Staffordshire, to the order of the
Prince of Wales, later King Edward VII.

This jubilee memorial mug is made of soft white porcelain
and is a half-pint cylindrical cup. In front it exhibits two
medallion portraits of the Queen, one as a girl, the other a
contemporary jubilee portrait, both wearing the crown. The
dates 1837 and 1887 are shown on a scroll which also bears the
letters VR, and the whole motif is surmounted by the Imperial
Crown.

Many of the mugs presented on this festive occasion must
still exist and be highly valued by their present owners; others
may turn up in unexpected places such as attics and lumber-
rooms when old houses are cleared. Hidden treasure is often
to be found when this happens.

King Edward VII was very interested in Doulton china and
later granted this company the privilege of using the prefix
'Royal' in their title. He was specially anxious that all his
subjects should enjoy and participate in the festivities sur-
rounding his Coronation, and one of his plans was for a special
free 'coronation dinner' to be given to the poor people of
London (some half a million in all at that time).

This was arranged throughout London. The plans included
entertainments and provision for each guest to be given an
earthenware beaker – which could be kept as a memento – for
his or her own use at the festive meal. The records of Royal
Doulton show that King Edward VII ordered 500,000 of
these earthenware beakers, decorated with portraits of the
King and Queen, surmounted with a crown, and on the
reverse side an inscription – 'Presented by His Majesty' sur-
rounded by a ribbon bearing 'The King's Coronation Dinner'.
These beakers, which are of cream-coloured china, with
multi-coloured decorations, measure 9·6cm. high. The
enthusiastic collector should not have too much trouble in
finding one and may be interested in press photographs of that

time showing the celebration dinners in progress with the
beakers on the tables.

Coronation mugs made especially for schoolchildren are, of
course, also much collected today, although they are usually of
indifferent quality compared with the specially commissioned
souvenir beakers; nevertheless they are historic mementoes
of past eras.

Souvenir china and eathenware objects are not, of course,
necessarily commemorative pieces, although these too can
make interesting collections. We are all familiar with plates,
jugs, cups, saucers, tea pots, etc. with 'A present from . . .'
printed on them. Many also have a view of the place in ques-
tion and these may have special interest as the views shown on
Victorian pieces, for example, have often changed almost
beyond recognition today.

*4. Commemorative mugs from Wedgwood that tell their own story. They
are made of black basalt*

It is strange how commemorative pieces such as those made for the Wembley Exhibition, the Festival of Britain, and even the Coronation of Queen Elizabeth II, so prolific at the time, disappear as if by magic after the events, and one wonders what has become of the pieces that were unsold among the floods of articles. Are they in store to be produced in a hundred years from now as true antiques? Or could we find them on market junk stalls or at jumble sales as 'out of date' items for a few pence perhaps, and then preserve them with one's own collection of older commemoratives to ripen with the years?

Wolverhampton Art Gallery and Museum has held several interesting exhibitions of souvenirs during the last few years, including 'Here's a Health Unto Their Majesties . . .' consisting of souvenirs from 1603–1953, in great variety, many of which were kindly lent by a number of public and private collectors.

Another of their exhibitions entitled 'A Present From . . .' consisted largely of seaside souvenirs, many of which were amusing trifles expressing the lighthearted mood of holidaymakers during the last hundred years or so. These were also lent by public and private collectors and were gay and amusing.

The Commemorative Collectors' Society has done much to foster interest in the whole subject since it was formed in 1971. This very lively and go-ahead society publishes periodical journals of great interest to collectors which contain illustrated features by well-known authorities on the subject of commemoratives, up-to-date news of new issues, news of meetings and events of the Society, 'Wanted' and 'For Sale' advertisements for members, and so on. Further particulars can be obtained from The Secretary, Mr Steven N. Jackson at 25 Ferndale Close, Long Eaton, Nottingham, NG10 3PA.

As mentioned before, the large numbers of commemorative items being issued in America to commemorate the bicentenary of the Declaration of Independence, will make a

5, 6. and 7. Amusing seaside souvenirs from an exhibition called 'A Present From . . .' given by the Wolverhampton Art Gallery and Museum

historic collection. Many of these are being made in Britain by
some of the finest manufacturers, and exported to the USA;
other European countries are also sending some fine contribu-
tions. Quantities of souvenirs for this important occasion are
also, of course, being made in America, so the choice for
collectors will be very varied.

8. *A copy of a print by John Binns dated 1818 of The American
Declaration of Independence. A limited edition of 1000 copies of the print
has been published by Mrs Caradoc Evans, Conway, North Wales*

9. *Wedgwood mugs commemorating the Prince of Wales' Investiture in 1969*

Another event which brought about the issue of some interesting commemorative pieces was the 1975 bi-centenary of the Royal Copenhagen Porcelain Company. This company has long been renowned for its exquisite ceramics, and their Christmas plates, made each year to celebrate the festive season, are famous.

In fact commemoratives from many parts of the world give the collector a wide variety of choice in this fascinating subject, marking as they do past and present events, and no doubt they will continue to do so in the future, and collectors of all ages, nationalities and tastes can find interest in this absorbing subject.

10. *These pieces were produced by Wedgwood to commemorate the wedding of Princess Anne and Captain Mark Phillips in 1973*

# 8 PRINTED EPHEMERA

Collecting printed ephemera is a hobby that anyone can afford. It usually consists of simple objects, the sorts of things that get discarded as rubbish by most housewives. These apparently insignificant items can be brought together in such a way that they form a valuable background to their period in social history. The late Dr John Johnson, printer to the University of Oxford, and one of the greatest known collectors in this field, had a collection of real historical value which is housed today in the Bodleian Library. It is studied by scholars from all over the world, who find it an invaluable source of information whatever their particular interest may be – politics, technology, social history, economics, costume, printing, illustrations.

The collection is also available to the general public for reference and study. There are newspapers and periodicals of all kinds, catalogues, posters, programmes, card and table games, playing cards, cigarette cards and packets, paper fans, coupons of all kinds, leaflets, pamphlets, postcards, envelopes, postage stamps and stationery in great variety, railway plans, timetables, political cartoons, strike notices and propaganda material of every kind, including some fine specimens from the period when suffragettes were on the warpath. There are also tickets of all kinds – such as bus, tram and train as well as tickets for sporting events and entertainments.

This collection also includes every kind of advertising material, food packages and labels, calendars, diaries, banknotes, share certificates, birthday and Christmas cards, Valentines, fireworks, matchboxes, badges, guides, maps, almanacs and prospectuses.

Average collectors would have neither the time nor the space to house such a quantity of material, but would probably take one category or period in time, of special personal interest, and even then would find this expanding as their knowledge increased.

A collection of bank notes for instance could be expanded to cover the entire world – in the same way as a stamp collection – or could be kept 'local'. Nor need this absorbing hobby be expensive. Many interesting notes can still be purchased for one pound or less, and in this way a collector can possess many miniature works of art – some of the best artists of the day being responsible for their design. The collector of bank notes is also free from the worry of whether or not he is buying a genuine article for it is, of course, against the law to produce false bank notes and the offence is punishable by confiscation and a prison sentence.

A useful book on the subject is *Collect British Bank Notes* edited by Colin Narbeth and published by Stanley Gibbons. It includes many interesting facts about what to look for when making a purchase for your collection. Gibbons sell several books on the subject and also have a library, which is available for the use of collectors, on their premises in London.

As paper money has existed in Great Britain since the reign of Charles I there is plenty of choice for the collector. He may collect any of the issues of the hundreds of private banks, many decorated with views of Old England. And there is also a huge range of Scottish and Irish notes, also as well as those of the Channel Islands and Isle of Man.

It can be great fun too to extend your collection to foreign bank notes which can be found in all shapes and sizes, and there is plenty of scope, whether your special interest is history, geography, or the artistic appeal of the notes. From a financial angle also you will actually be 'saving money' while enjoying the hobby, which is always satisfactory.

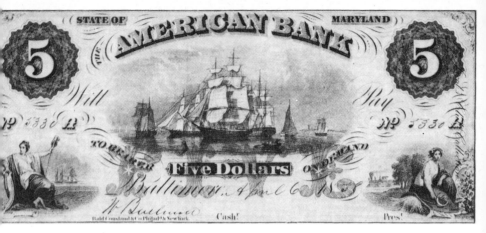

1. *A 19th-century five-dollar note from the State of Maryland*

As a point of interest, the Bank of England was founded in 1694, issuing its bank notes in that year. They were then written by hand on ordinary paper, a practice which of course led to forgery. So in 1697 watermarked paper was introduced for Bank of England notes and no one else is allowed to use it.

On the subject of collecting old magazines and publications I understand that the Vintage Magazine Shop at the Cambridge Circus end of Earlham Street, London, has a good selection. There are also some stalls outside this shop, one of which specializes in American comics, another in science fiction and original artwork. Children's books are also much collected, and it saddens me to think that in the course of spring-cleaning clearances in the nursery at my home my *Girl's Own* annuals, *Playbox* and other familiar nursery reading matter of bygone years were disposed of. These would now fetch a tidy sum if one could bring oneself to part with such nostalgic treasures. Any young mother reading this should think twice before throwing away discarded nursery books, especially if they are in good condition, for Dougal and Florence and the friends of the Magic Roundabout or indeed Tom and Jerry may be of historic interest to future generations! Who can tell?

I recently visited an exhibition at our local museum entitled 'Victorian Miscellany' which included many interesting items of bygone days, including old passports, a will and some household bills, the prices on which were quite startling by today's standards. There were also dance programmes and a variety of invitations to social occasions. Below is illustrated an invitation to the Coronation of Queen Victoria from a collection of royal invitations and of programmes of soirées held at such places as Buckingham Palace and Windsor Castle. These were exhibited at a recent Chelsea Antiques Fair, and are no doubt greatly valued by their owner.

2. *An invitation to Queen Victoria's Coronation, June 28, 1838*

THE
INTERNATIONAL
HORSE
SHOW
OLYMPIA
LONDON
JUNE 5-15
1909

*3. An early 20th-century postcard from the Frank Staff collection*

Christmas cards, Valentines and birthday cards all have their fascination as the years roll by and there was a fine exhibition of postcards – Fifty Years of Postcards – at the Victoria and Albert Museum to celebrate the centenary of the postcard, a few years ago. The subjects are legion for the collector of old postcards, who may specialise in old views of the seaside and country places, now changed beyond recognition, or in bathing belles of the past in unbelievable creations; in stage or screen personalities or Royalty; in trains, ships and aeroplanes of another generation. We wonder which of the many excellent coloured postcards on sale today will interest the next generation. Will our times interest and amuse them fifty or a hundred years from now; perhaps they will prefer to look forwards and not backwards and the 'good old days' will be out of fashion.

Christmas cards will surely get scarcer as postage increases and this is sad as the pretty cards dropping through the letterbox, from friends and relatives who we seldom see in these busy times, form a link that it is hard to sever, and greetings cards of all kinds have become today's substitute for the once popular art of letter-writing. Of recent years 'Get Well' cards, 'Congratulations' for achievements and different occasions, have been growing in numbers and variety. Are they to be among the antiques of the future? And will today's humorous cards raise a smile a hundred years from now?

Cigarette cards have been collected with enthusiasm since the last war. The boys and girls of the early 1900s hoarded albums of them, which were 'swopped' with young friends until sets were completed. These collections, discarded by their owners years ago, are now valuable and fetch high prices at auction where they are purchased by venerable collectors, some of whom were no doubt the schoolboy cigarette card enthusiasts of pre-1914 war days. What is there today that takes their place? Certainly not trading stamps, or coupons.

There are said to be between 5,000 and 10,000 different series of British cigarette cards alone in existence. Many are of a high standard of design and colour printing, as well as being informative, and it is little wonder there is a craze for these interesting 'bygones'.

I understand that the military uniform series is among the most valuable. These were on cards from about 1895–1902/3, and prices today vary from about 10p to £40 each according to rarity and condition. Specialised auction sales are held. Two organisations are most helpful to a would-be collector: The London Cigarette Card Company, 34 Wellesley Road, London, W11, and The Cartophilic Society of Great Britain, Secretary Mr E. F. Pressly, Clewin, Maidenhead Road, Windsor.

Two excellent books by the famous collector, Frank Staff – *The Picture Postcard and Its Origins* and *The Valentine and Its Origins* are both well illustrated and full of interesting information. They are obtainable from the reference section of most public libraries and make delightful and informative reading for collectors and others.

Old newspapers and magazines can also be fascinating but, strangely enough, collectors of these are few and far between. As nothing reflects a period better than the newspaper, so it should be valued as a historical record of events in our ever-changing world. The advertisements alone illustrate how social customs change.

In this field, of course, it would be necessary to specialise or one's collection would become impossibly bulky, but the choice of subjects is legion. Royal occasions might appeal to some while the continuing conquest of space or sporting events might appeal to others. (Programmes of these are especially collectable.) The collector will develop his own particular interest in pursuing this absorbing hobby.

One is unlikely to find copies of very early newspapers for sale, although opportunities do occasionally occur to acquire historic issues at auctions. Antiquarian bookshops can sometimes help and, although they need searching for, interesting old newspapers can still be bought for quite a modest sum.

Just to illustrate the possible value of old magazines and newspapers, a friend of mine spring cleaning her husband's study came across a large pile of back numbers, in consecutive order, of a scientific magazine. She offered them to the appropriate society and received a cheque for £800!

Reading the personal column in my Sunday newspaper

MAY PLENTY SMILE ON CHRISTMAS

A MERRY CHRISTMAS TO YOU

WISH YOU GOOD CHEER
AND A
HAPPY NEW YEAR

*4. and 5.* Left, *Victorian Christmas cards from Hallmark Cards.* Above, *cigarette cards sold by auction at Knight, Frank and Rutley*

recently, I saw collectors advertising for 'Autograph letters, old ship's logs, diaries and journals'. In the same column another advertiser wanted 'War diaries, letters, documents and regimental histories' and a third stated 'Wanted by collector, old beer labels, will purchase collections or single labels'.

Certainly printed ephemera offers endless opportunities and a wide selection of 'souvenirs' or 'rubbish', according to the way you look at it, and if you have the space and courage to store it, you might find one day that it is worth its weight in gold.

6. *John Hassall's famous 1925 poster here reproduced on a mirror*

# 9 MEMENTOES OF A CHANGING WORLD

Fashion is the oldest of the arts and it is known that primitive man adorned his body with dye and other forms of ornament before history began; also many tombs of the ancients reveal jewellery and other personal ornaments made from metal or stone which have survived the ages and tell their own tale.

Today we add jewellery and ornamental fashion accessories after clothing our bodies, but it appears that the reverse procedure was true of our early ancestors, to whom clothing came second to decoration, illustrating the fundamental instinct of mankind for personal adornment.

Information about fashion through the centuries can be found in a number of excellent books and some museums now have fine displays of historical costumes showing the changing fashions over the years. Perhaps no change has been more drastic than today's, when long hair and bright colours are back in favour with men, and women, for the first time in our history, deck themselves out in trousers. Decorative although many of these new fashions are, and suitable for today's way of life, they do not compare favourably with the feminine charm of the dainty silks and muslins worn a hundred and more years ago. One is at a loss to know which, if any, of the man-made fabrics of today will survive to represent the 1970s as antiques of the future.

For the average collector however interested in fashion, small accessories made of a durable substance are likely to be practical. For example, purses and handbags, which illustrate the taste of succeeding generations in a variety of ways can be very interesting collectors' items.

Both men and women originally used purses to carry money, though it will be found that few have survived that were in use before the Victorian era. It will also be noticed that old purses are much smaller than those we use today. Ladies and gentlemen of fashion in the eighteenth and nineteenth centuries, for example, seldom needed to carry much money as the goods that now fill our trolleys and shopping baskets requiring payment in cash were once delivered to the door, where a weekly or monthly settlement took place. The items were ordered or selected by the housewife and were then entered into the tradesmen's books by hand, for weekly or monthly settlement. Incidentally, these small account books are eminently collectable, illustrating as they do the vast changes in prices and commodities over the last three or four generations. They had hard covers, the shopkeeper's name and address was usually embossed in gilt on the front, and there was a little cut-out window for the customer's name. Alas, most of the privately owned 'butchers, bakers and candlestick makers' who made shopping such a personal matter have long since disappeared.

To return to purses, most of those dating from the early nineteenth century are made of crochet, netting, knitting or are woven on some attractive fabric. Many were beaded with tiny beads which made them strong and also very decorative. The traditional and most characteristic shape was the 'long purse'. These were also known as 'miser's purses', 'stocking purses' and 'ring purses', and were fashionable until the end of the last century. This shape of purse was also used in the Middle Ages, but was then usually made of leather and it is thought the name 'miser's purse' indicated that they did not hold much money. The coins were inserted in a slit in the centre and held in place by pushing down two rings which secured the contents. The purse could then be worn slung over the belt. (See the illustration opposite.)

Purses with rigid metal frames and snap fasteners became popular during the nineteenth century and were sometimes

1. A collection of purses made in the late 19th and early 20th centuries. It includes, bottom far right, a whole ermine skin miser's purse. From the Ronald Bayman collection exhibited at a recent Chelsea Antiques Fair

2. *Some Edwardian and Victorian belt buckles, including those worn by nurses*

known as chatelaine purses; other purses were designed with a drawstring like tiny 'Dorothy' bags.

Note-cases or wallets were not required in those far off days, but metal sovereign purses became popular towards the end of the nineteenth century. These were of gold or silver and worn on a gentleman's watch chain. The sovereigns and half-sovereigns were kept in place by two horseshoe springs inside; one in the lid for half-sovereigns, and one in the other section for sovereigns. These purses are now much sought-after by collectors and are liable to be quite expensive, especially if made of gold.

Handbags are usually made of more durable material than purses, especially in various leathers, and they can be bulky in a collection. Evening bags, on the other hand, made of silk, velvet, petit point, beaded or embroidered, and in good condition, can make charming collectors' pieces. In 1914 leather handbags were first worn hung from the arm by a handle or strap; the natural extension of this idea is today's shoulder bag which will perhaps one day be a collectors' item of the 60s and 70s. Unfortunately these bags are often made of plastic and have to hold so many bulky everyday objects that they are seldom discarded in any condition for collecting.

Buckles, buttons, belts, badges and hat pins are other dress accessories that are practicable collectors' items and all hold their own special interest.

3. *A selection of Victorian ornaments which might have been worn in the popular fashion of that time – centred on a black velvet neck band*

Antique shoe buckles were made in a great variety of styles and a fabulous collection of some 1300 eighteenth century buckles was recently presented by Lady Maufe to form part of the collection of art treasures at Kenwood House in London. The range of this collection, believed to be the largest and most comprehensive in existence, is so great that it presents an opportunity for the would-be collector or student of costume to study the whole subject. Many of the buckles are of silver and carry hallmarks and maker's names which date them reliably; others are of paste, cut steel, jet (for mourning buckles), enamel or pinchbeck. There are also some made with garnets, other semi-precious stones, and a great variety of materials. At one time, when buckles were the usual fastening for shoes, and also worn on belts and hats, there were over a hundred master-buckle makers in England, employing several thousand people. The buckles made of valuable substances and of more elaborate design were worn by the fashionable and wealthy ladies and their beaux, while more sober merchants and craftsmen wore silver. Contemporary prints and paintings show that simple buckles were also included in a servants' livery – as, of course, were silver buttons, usually marked with the arms or crest of their employers.

Livery buttons of all kinds are collectable items today, whether they belonged to a nobleman's estate or come from the uniforms of railway officials, postmen or other public servants. There are of course quantities of delightful buttons, both old and new and made in a variety of fascinating materials that the collector can find and he or she may find P. Peacock's *Buttons for the Collector* a useful aid. In the United States where there has long been a great enthusiasm for button collecting, there is an active National Button Society at 7940 Montgomery Avenue, Elkins Park, Philadelphia.

Belts have varied over the centuries and the flexible silver belts worn at the turn of the last century provide a fairly fresh field for the collector; so too do the lovely silver belt buckles worn by hospital nurses, though I have been told that these are now frowned on by some hospital authorities and may soon not be worn. Scarcity, however, should enhance the value of these lovely objects as they gain status as antiques, and the collector could also extend his interest to nurses' badges which have been made in a changing variety of attractive designs.

Hat pins were fashionable from the end of the Victorian era until the First World War when cartwheel and other splendid

*4. Some jet and black glass hat pins which were very fashionable at the beginning of this century. This group was on display at the 40th Chelsea Antiques Fair*

5. *A print dated 1841 showing English fashions and now collectable accessories*

'picture' hats were the vogue. These formidable pins, although not yet the required hundred years old to make them 'qualify' as antiques, are well worth collecting. At a recent Chelsea Antiques Fair a collection of over 2000 hat pins from all over the world was exhibited. They had been lent by a private collector and the variety was amazing. I was specially interested in some which showed a strong Scottish influence in the Art Nouveau style. They were made of hallmarked silver (which dated them authentically) and were set with amethysts and citrine. Incidentally, Scottish silver jewellery such as brooches and kilt pins would make a delightful and valuable collection. The traditional designs set with Scottish semi-precious stones in silver cannot fail to appeal to future generations.

Regimental badges are also very collectable, especially since the structure of the British Army has undergone many changes since the last war. The old historic cap badges of traditional regiments are becoming scarce, and are well worth looking for as no more will be made in those once familiar designs that often represented incidents in famous battles or achievements in military history. Militaria generally is a fine collector's subject, but too big to include here. It is, however, well worth hunting for badges, divisional signs and other small insignia off the uniforms of the Navy, Army and Air Force in this ever-changing world.

# 10   THE DINING ROOM, THEN AND NOW

The social and domestic changes that have taken place since the beginning of this century have been the cause of an entirely new outlook and arrangement in home surroundings and a drastic curtailment in today's way of life.

The lavish meals once cooked below stairs to be served on large family tables are prepared no more. The spacious dining rooms which were considered necessary for gracious living have disappeared from an average home, where simplicity of decor and labour-saving furnishing are the present vogue.

Snowy damask table linen on which crystal glass sparkled, silver gleamed, and beautiful china harmonised with the surroundings, is seldom seen today. Nowadays dining rooms are not necessarily part of the design in modern architectural planning, and meals are less formal except on special occasions. A dining area off the living room or in a section of a modern fitted kitchen is now a generally accepted way of saving valuable space and labour.

With these changes many lovely objects that were in daily use fifty or sixty years ago have become collectors' items. Gone are the days when many willing hands were available to clean silver, polish furniture and brass, cook elaborate meals, or wait at table, handing the beautiful silver dishes to the family and guests with appropriate servers for every course.

A dinner table in a prosperous Georgian home, for example, held weighty silver items such as candelabra, a number of tureens, silver salvers, trays, coffee and tea pots, jugs, a wine cooler and a lavish selection of spoons and forks, special scoops, ladles, gravy spoons, caddy and mote spoons, cutlery knife rests, condiment sets, cruets, menu holders, etc.

1. *Dining room table, chairs and silverware of the 1760s*

The Victorians introduced an even greater variety of basic cutlery, such as fish knives and forks, fish servers, fruit knives and special forks for pickles, bread, etc., silver bordered bread boards for the table, entrée dishes, cake baskets and stands, and various other elegant silver tableware.

Coasters and wine labels were also the vogue, and all these small silver items and many more are now recognised as collectable, without involving too much expense, as Victorian and Edwardian silver is still plentiful. Hallmarks prove its age, and although it may not yet have passed the required hundred years to qualify officially as 'antique', it will not be long before it does so; therefore these small decorative silver objects could be a good investment as 'tomorrow's antiques'.

The dining chairs of our forefathers were well made and comfortable and sets of these are fetching a good price today

2. *Knife rests of various materials, styles and periods. From Sara Morse's unique collection exhibited at a Chelsea Antiques Fair*

for use in other parts of the house. It is a great mistake to divide a set, as if it can eventually be sold together it fetches considerably more than if sold separately. Large polished dining tables are now usually in demand for board room tables, but unfortunately many of them have been cut up for their solid timber and converted into smaller pieces of furniture or used for repairs and restoration. Victorian and Edwardian sideboards have suffered a similar fate; only large homes have the space to accommodate these hefty pieces, which once groaned under all the paraphernalia used at family meals, but which have been sold during the last thirty years for the proverbial song. Not long ago, for example, I saw a large Victorian sideboard made of fine mahogany sold at a country auction for seventy-five pence, and the carving from the back of another one was cut off and used for an attractive bedhead.

3. A George III Warwick cruet on scroll and scallop supports made in
1763 by John Delmester

What do we use today at meal times that will survive to be antiques of the future? Looking through a modern furniture catalogue, it is difficult to say. Certainly some of the delightful present-day casseroles used for cooking and brought straight to the table are most decorative as well as being practical. Also much of the modern tableware is well designed and made of fine quality bone china so its value will undoubtedly increase. One can think of a score or more British makers of ceramics alone, whose merchandise is equal in quality and design to much that we value today as antique.

Modern hand-woven rugs on polished floors are also timeless, and the austere lines of today's stick-back chairs, round tables with a waxed surface showing the beautiful grain of wood (and mercifully not requiring polish!) all seem to me to have great merit and are likely to appeal to future generations, who may also have to consider labour-saving devices.

*4. A condiment set of the 1970s designed by Alex Styles of Garrard and Co Ltd, London W1*

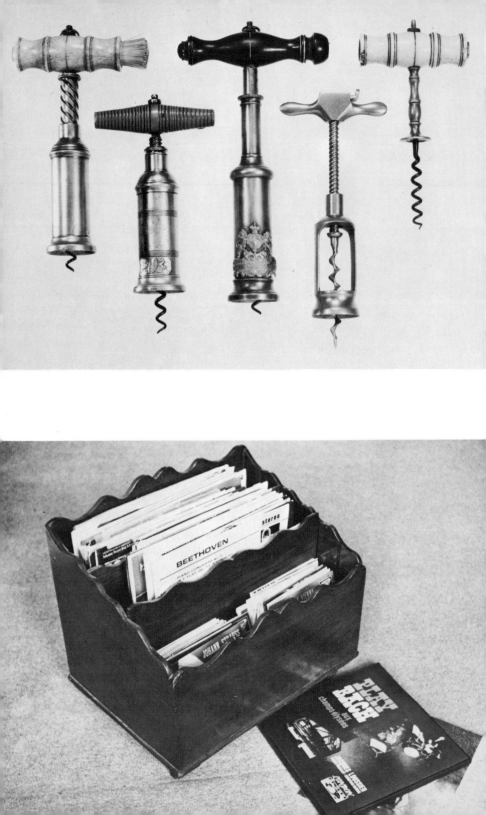

5. *and* 6. Left, above, *an interesting selection of 18th- and 19th-century corkscrews.* Below, *new life for an antique cutlery tray*

7. *and* 8. Right, above, *modern oven-to-table ware from the Wedgwood Group.* Below, *a decanter, tray and four goblets in 18ct. gold from Gerald Benny*

Table mats, too, may one day be looked upon as antiques and these could then be collectable, as heat resistant surfaces on modern tables are fast making mats or table-cloths redundant. Sparkling glass continues to be used for wine and other drinks and much of today's glass is of such superb quality and workmanship, that its owners can reasonably treasure it for the future.

The quality of the best modern glass is good, but of course its survival is risky, and it is quite wonderful how much antique glass is still intact.

The now far-off era of oak furnishing with its simple lines, lack of artificial stain or polish, and its mellow natural colour, blends well with modern hand-woven fabrics and contemporary colour schemes; consequently it has made a real comeback after some years in the doldrums. The old oak dresser excels as a background for gleaming pewter, copper or brass, and has no modern counterpart. It is cheering to know, however, that a number of fine individual craftsmen are now using their skills to create furniture masterpieces with a future.

As in some of the other crafts mentioned in the first section of this book, it will be found that many examples of craftsman-made furniture, designed in the present idiom, stand out as fine twentieth century work, so these too may well qualify to become museum pieces in the years to come.

# 11 DESK TREASURES, COMMUNI-CATIONS AND SMOKING ANTIQUES

The Victorians were compulsive correspondents and much of their time was taken up at writing tables or desks composing letters, notes, invitations and entries in diaries in which they faithfully recorded the day-to-day happenings and their inmost thoughts. These very personal chronicles were entered in a careful copper-plate hand and give us a clear insight into the character of the writer and the life of the times.

Many of these diaries had locking clasps to guard against prying eyes, and reading my own great grandmother's diary, which was in a simple exercise book bound in a soft green velvet cover, I realised that it was a source of comfort to the writer to record her joys and sorrows in this way, and reading it gave me a rather special way of becoming acquainted with her. This privilege is unlikely to be given to future generations as desk diaries are seldom kept today. Perhaps the custom should be revived and these volumes could then become antiques for the future. The slim books called diaries which we carry round will not make very interesting reading at some future date, simply recording as they do business appointments, hair-do's, dentists and other brief details of our present life style, which are unlikely to introduce us as individuals to our great-grandchildren (for which, who knows, they may be truly thankful!).

In the same way other accessories that equipped the writing tables of our forebears have either changed in character or are no longer in use. Many of these items, however, are collectable today. For example, inkstands and inkpots of every shape and size have largely disappeared from use. Even the handsome desk furnishing in an executive office has been replaced by modern gadgets. Will the coloured telephones, calculators, dictaphones and similar equipment be collectable as future antiques? Early telephones are already much in demand by interior decorators and for theatrical and other performances.

Our modern requisites are functional and not often designed to charm us like the pretty materials from which writing accessories were once made. For example, the papier-mâché blotters decorated with painted flowers and inlaid with mother of pearl, or the handsome inkstands with pen trays and cut glass or porcelain bottles to hold black and coloured inks, the stationery cabinets, many of which were also of papier-mâché en suite with the blotters; while other desk sets were made from choice woods with silver or brass corners and inlay. Tunbridge ware or tartan-covered stamp boxes were popular, also ivory or agate penholders and coloured quills. The earlier pounce pots with perforated lids for sprinkling sand were in use before blotting paper was general. Seals and sealing wax were essential until the introduction of the gummed envelope in 1840, and so many other delightful etceteras must have added pleasure to writing elegant and newsy letters.

Also in 1840 Rowland Hill inaugurated his now famous 'Penny Post', and when gummed postage stamps superseded sealing wax this important introduction of course gave birth to the now world-wide hobby of philately.

Paperweights are still useful and many modern examples may well stand the test of time to become future antiques. They can be so varied and interesting. In my home I use large sea shells to anchor my papers in the 'pending' file, and I have even seen heavy pebbles from the sea shore painted in oils with local views, which make charming and practical weights. A walk down Bond Street or Fifth Avenue, however, would tempt the collector to acquire lovely modern paperweights made of glass or alabaster, quartz, ormolu, bronze and many other decorative substances.

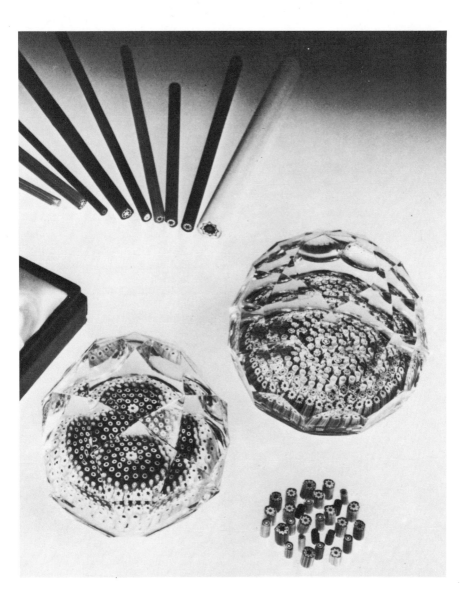

1. A selection of Millefioré paperweights based on techniques used by craftsmen since the 1840s. No two designs are the same. The glass canes are used to form the designs

2. *Antique paperweights*

3. *Elegant silver and agate paper knives by Jocelyn Burton shown at the 'Loot' exhibition at London's Goldsmiths' Hall*

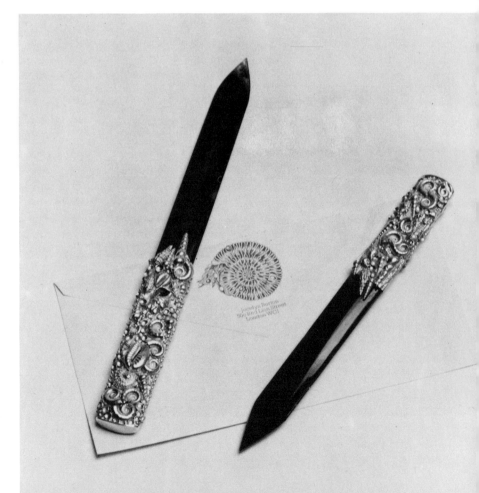

4. *Collectable writing accessories seen at London's Hampstead Antiques Emporium*

Strathearn Glass of Crieff and Whitefriars Glass of Harrow now both produce Millefioré glass weights at reasonable prices. The craftsmanship and design are comparable with those made famous in France in the 1840s which now sell in the sale rooms at several hundreds or even thousands of pounds.

The knowledge and skill required in the intricate production of decorative glass paperweights is most complicated and the mind boggles at the ingenuity and dexterity involved over the years in creating these fascinating baubles from molten glass.

The numerous small silver objects associated with letter-writing are all collectable and until the telephone became a general method of communication early this century, letter writing on elegant stationery persisted as a social necessity.

Writing boxes or lap desks were once in general use as an alternative to special writing tables. These folding boxes open out to form a slope on which to write and are most useful today when space is often a problem. They usually contain a pen tray and ink bottles, and the lower portion often includes a secret drawer. Careful tapping, which should locate the spring will release it. One always hopes to find something interesting hidden there, which is intriguing, although I have never been lucky enough to do so.

These boxes are craftsman-made of solid timber and are frequently brass-bound with sunken brass handles, or inlaid with some decorative substance such as mother of pearl. It is a delight for a guest to find one for his use in a spare bedroom and as they are still comparatively plentiful and reasonably priced, they are worth looking for.

Old wireless sets are now considered collectable by some enthusiasts, along with early cameras, gramophones, type-writers, and sewing machines; but whether the television sets of the seventies will be considered worth collecting would seem extremely doubtful.

Our present-day good quality biro and fountain pens may well be antiques for the future, as many of them are well made, decorative and comparatively durable. Apart from these, and the paperweights mentioned above, writing accessories have largely disappeared, with the possible exception of paper knives, which can be collectable whether belonging to the past or present eras and still give scope for creative artist-craftsmen of the seventies. (See the illustration on page 122.)

Smoking is another custom that through the centuries has attracted many accessories. Ashtrays, old and new, could form an interesting collection, although they have increased in numbers and variety this century since cigarette smoking has largely superseded the pipe. Decorative cigarette cases and holders were the vogue in the 1920s but are no longer fash-ionable, so are quite collectable today. The cardboard packets and cigarette lighters in present use seem unlikely to hold much interest for the future, but as old labelled match boxes are now collected, one cannot tell. Vesta cases once worn on

5. *A modern cigarette box designed by Gordon Hodgson and a prize winner in The Design Centre's 'Silver for the Seventies' competition*

the watch chains of our grandfathers and used before safety matches were invented now fetch a good price and who knows – perhaps smoking may become an obsolete custom and all these things could then be looked upon as curios in the years to come.

Many of the subjects discussed in this chapter emphasize the fascination of the passing of time and change of customs lends enchantment to collecting even the simplest everyday objects.

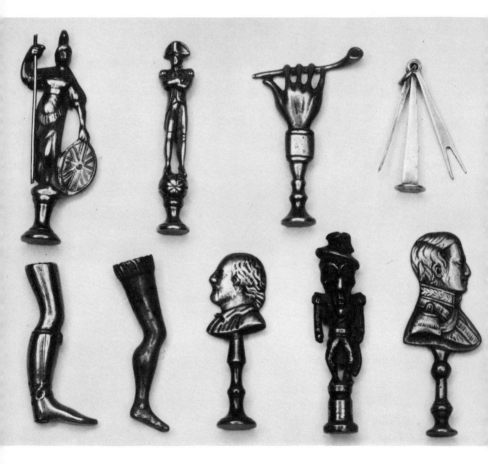

6. *Part of an exhibition of antique tobacco stoppers shown at a Chelsea Antiques Fair*

# 12  CHANGES IN THE KITCHEN

Kitchen bygones tell us a tale of social and domestic history through the centuries, and some museums have acquired interesting household utensils from days gone by and display them in an appropriate setting. The quantity of such kitchenware available to the collector, however, is still plentiful and some pieces can be found at moderate prices.

The simple beauty of milk churns, cans and pitchers, terra cotta bread crocks, ornamental pie dishes, copper jelly moulds and saucepans, brass scales with their solid little weights, the tinware circular spice boxes, wood or stone pestle and mortars, baskets and the many articles made of treen, such as wooden bowls, rolling pins and spoons, butter prints and pats, and the spacious kitchen table itself that was scrubbed to whiteness with fine sand, all have a very special appeal today. The toasting forks, kettles, pots and pans of our ancestors, and countless other useful objects are redolent with homely usage and a universal timeless way of life.

These domestic items were once basic necessities, each with a useful purpose to perform, and this lends them the special character of times gone by, when today's so-called convenience foods, in disposable plastic containers, were still undreamt of.

Today's kitchens may be more functional, hygienic and labour saving, but they have now lost the simple beauty and homely character that for generations made a kitchen the centre of daily living. Fortunately domestic items of the past had lasting qualities, whether for use in the kitchen, dairy or laundry, and they were often handed down from mother to

1. *A hoop-back Windsor armchair made in the first half of the 19th century and used in country kitchens*

2. *A Georgian copper hob kettle with a loop handle*

daughter, or even grand-daughter. Their original cost was minimal compared with today's prices, but they were well made and durable, and are often most decorative, so these everyday articles are collectable to anyone who is interested in the home life of the past.

Although many of them could have been used in almost any kitchen, all nations have their characteristic domestic equipment, and this widens the possibility for collectors to add variety and interest to their hobby when they travel abroad.

Britain's change to the metric system in 1975 will date scales and measuring cups, packages and containers, cookery and recipe books, in the future, as emphatically as the hallmarks on silver, which will greatly assist the coming generations to identify these things as made before or after this big change took place.

Drastic changes of materials too, have also come about during this century with the introduction of gas and electric equipment of all kinds, stainless steel, plastic, formica, enamel, aluminium, fibre-glass, non-stick pans and many other useful inventions, so one is at a loss to know what will survive the centuries to mark our times in the kitchen, and become antiques for the future.

Looking around shops that sell good quality cooking utensils and tableware, for example, one is struck by the fact that so much of their stock is modelled on the old classic shapes, even if they are made in different materials today. Perhaps fondue sets and ice-cream making or barbecue equipment will find their way into tomorrow's antique shops as belonging to the Elizabeth II period. I like to think that some of the best quality ovenware and casseroles that we find such a boon today will survive the years, as many of them are really decorative as well as a practical way to cook and serve food, retaining all its goodness without wasting fuel or labour. Also they have the advantage of being colourful and durable and can act as vegetable or other serving dishes without necessarily having to match the fine dinner service that may probably be rather delicate for everyday use. Illustrated below are a selection of flan cases in contemporary design that may well be collectors' pieces in the years to come.

The early Victorian era saw the beginnings of prepared foods and domestic commodities packaged in attractive containers. For example, the pictorial lids of pots which originally contained bear grease used on the hair, are now highly valued. Later these pots were made to contain savoury pastes and

3. *Flan cases from Worcester Royal Porcelain Co Ltd*

many of them were decorated with fine quality colour printing of interesting views or famous people. They have been enthusiastically collected for many years and some specimens can fetch very high prices at auction today.

4. *A selection of pot lids.* Top, *Felix Edward Pratt the maker of pot lids.* Left, *Harriet Beacher Stowe.* Right, *the Duke of Wellington*

*5. Mustard pots in various shapes and sizes*

Enterprising Victorian businessmen extended the idea of attractive packaging to bottled sauces, relishes, pickles, soups, cleaning and cooking aids. Prior to this era the housewife was expected to preserve all her own food such as bottled fruit, jams, pickles and sauces, grind her own spices, make home-made polishes, cleaners and washing material in addition to her cosmetics, and deal with her countless other domestic duties. It is small wonder that ready-made aids were most acceptable. The containers of some of these make amusing collections; for example, Colman's mustard pots, illustrated above. Powdered mustard had been introduced by an enterprising lady in 1720 and was commercially produced in London by Keens in 1742. In 1814 Jeremiah Colman founded the famous Norwich firm of that name and eventually took over Keens and other small firms marketing mustard. Mustard had grown wild in quantities in East Anglia since Roman times, but with the introduction of it in powdered form and when it was also easily available commercially, mustard pots of all kinds became a usual item on the table.

Colman's were one of the many enterprising firms that saw the advertising potential of selling their products in the decorative pots which now make amusing collectors' items. Packets and tins of these early days were not so durable, so few have survived although collectors of pictorial biscuit tins are enthusiastic about their subject.

Advertising really took hold of the commercial world on both sides of the Atlantic during the Victorian era and promotional material of all kinds to advertise their wares by countless manufacturers was produced. These items were often intended to become interesting souvenirs and are still collectable. The same, no doubt, applies to advertising material of today. For example, in a hundred years from now the plastic novelties in our cornflake packets, the fancy jam jars, sauce, milk and squash bottles, coke tins, tea and biscuits cards and quantities of other advertising paraphernalia, may be of considerable interest and indicate our domestic habits to future collectors.

6. and 7. Kitchen and laundry implements of the seventeenth century, left, contrast interestingly with functional stainless steel kitchen equipment of the 1970s, above

# 13 HOBBIES, GAMES, AND PASTIMES

Anyone deciding to collect old parlour games will be drawn into an absorbing subject for research. Indoor games and pastimes played an important part in social life during the Georgian and Victorian eras, and some of these are making a real come-back today and are becoming rival leisure pursuits to watching television which, after all, is an unsociable if absorbing occupation. The game of draughts, for example, is known to have been played by the Romans, and pieces very similar to our present-day draughtsmen have been found in the ancient tombs in Egypt of 2000–1000 BC. Chess is believed to have originated in the Far East and it is thought to have been brought to Europe by warriors from the Crusades. Mah Jong, too, is reputed to have been played in China for over a thousand years and the pieces from a good set are magically beautiful and most collectable, as are some chessmen, examples of which are illustrated opposite. Modern chess sets made by fine designer-craftsmen today can be works of art that add enormously to the pleasure of the game, and will doubtless be antiques of the future. Dominoes is an historic game, thought to have been played in Italy in the seventeenth and eighteenth centuries, while playing cards appear to have come to Europe from the East in the fourteenth century, and to have been popular all over the Continent, although they did not conform to any standard until around the beginning of the eighteenth century. The signs on them and the numbers in the packs varied considerably from country to country. Italy seems to have been the first European country to refer to playing cards, after which the French

1. *and* 2. Above, *part of the Greygoose collection of single chessmen lent for a Chelsea Antiques Fair.* Below, *a contemporary chess set and board by* Stuart Devlin

followed with their own version and it is interesting to note that playing cards used in England, especially the designs of the court cards, are based on the original French kings and queens, and in fact have preserved the curious form of dress and quaintness of the original French court cards to this day. English playing cards also derive their symbols of Hearts, Spades, Diamonds and Clubs from the French, whereas other European countries have used other signs to signify the different suits.

The first known reference to playing cards in England is a statute in 1464 forbidding them to be imported, which was no doubt to protect their production in this country, which had then begun. It was not until 1628, however, that Charles I granted a charter to the Worshipful Company of Makers of Playing Cards which led to a customs duty on all imported cards.

There was strong religious prejudice against them on the Continent, where they were described as the 'invention of the devil', but Anne of Cleves was one of the first to introduce them into the English court and their popularity rapidly grew. The earliest English cards were uncoloured and examples of these can be seen in the British Museum, circa 1675. Similar types of cards persisted until about 1800, after which they became varied, and collectors do not need to search for whole packs; even one or two old playing cards can start a hobby that can take one all over the world, and some excellent books have been written on the subject. Many present-day playing cards are so decorative that they may be worth collecting now with an eye on the future.

Most indoor games went out of fashion with the coming of radio and television, but the trend is now growing for parlour games to return to popularity. The Design Centre in the Haymarket held an exhibition of recently-designed games, and Asprey's in Bond Street have opened a Games Room where they report a brisk demand for table games, many of which are made with the fine workmanship and materials of earlier times.

3. A collection of old playing cards, the round ones coming from the East

Parlour games of all kinds were very popular in Britain in the Georgian era and many charming games tables were made for the purpose. Opposite is illustrated an elegant example which could be used for such games as chess, backgammon and draughts and had drawers to hold the various pieces, cards and counters. There was even a workbag underneath for needlework which, all through the ages, has been a most popular pastime with the ladies. Today, after a lapse of some years, needlework has made an interesting comeback with a fresh and stimulating sense of colour and design. There is now a lively approach to different textures and stitches, incorporating the traditional methods with today's concepts. Much of this is very collectable and expressive of the seventies. If framed to preserve the work, as were the samplers and other old pieces of needlework, some contemporary pieces will no doubt survive to become antiques, expressing the impact of our era as vividly as the samplers of old introduce us to the gentler spirit of their age.

*4. Some old sewing boxes and needlework tools from London's Hampstead Antique Emporium*

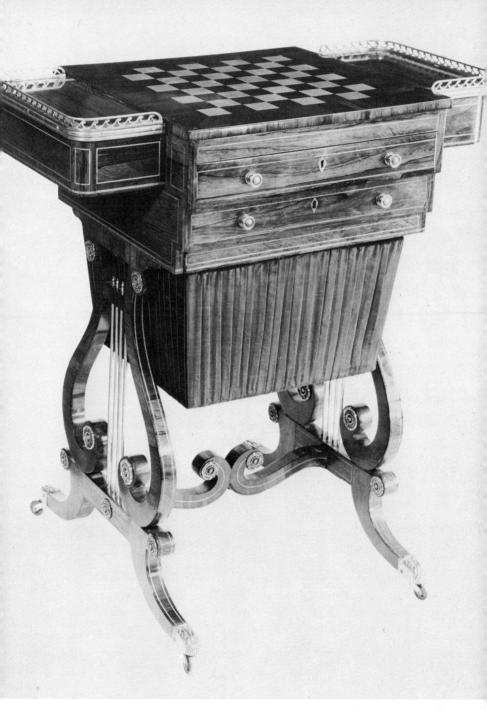

5. A Regency games table exhibited at a Chelsea Antiques Fair by Michael Foster. The centre section lifts out to reveal chess and backgammon boards

6. *A horse-drawn ambulance made before the First World War*

Children's toys of every period evoke the feeling of their times with surprising accuracy. The picture puzzles which once taught children botany and other educational subjects now depict the space age and power games. Steam trains and toy soldiers of the past are already valuable antiques. What, we wonder, will represent our times so eloquently a hundred years from now?

A recent exhibition held in London, entitled 'Play, Now and Then', was thought-provoking. It was organised by the Crafts Advisory Committee at their Waterloo Place Gallery and showed a collection of historic toys on loan from the London and Bethnal Green Museums. For example, a giant display of dolls' houses, appropriately furnished, toy buses and trains, dolls, clowns, golliwogs and rocking horses from 1880 onwards. In contrast to these were contemporary toys such as wooden animal puzzles, rattles in the modern idiom; robust

7. Left, *a large doll made between 1860 and 1870.* Centre, *this one was made around 1830.* Right, *an Edwardian fashion doll*

lorries, aeroplanes, barges and sailing boats made by present-day craftsmen; they also showed fibre-glass and plastic toys, and soft cuddly animals made of real fur. All these things were well made, and if kept away from destructive nursery treatment, will possibly become collectors' pieces at some future date. In fact children's toys and games of every age could fill a whole volume, as collectors' items.

Collecting children's books has already been touched on in Chapter 8, but of course all types of books are collectable. As in all forms of collecting, it is well to specialise; for example, on books by a favourite author, or dealing with a subject you find particularly interesting. The search will always be enjoyable and there are bargains still to be had. If you feel you have a really rare old book in your possession you can always send or take it to the British Museum and ask their advice. A friend of mine did this with an old book she very nearly threw away. The Museum advised her where to get the book valued and as a result she was able to sell it for £400!

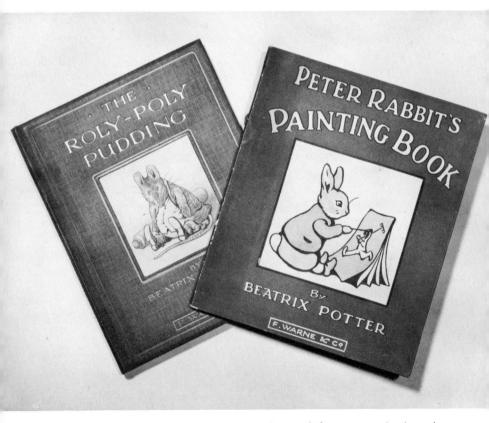

8. *First editions of Beatrix Potter books on exhibition at an Antiquarian Book Fair in London*

# 14   FIXTURES AND FITTINGS

Everyday objects in today's changing world can become interesting collectors' items for the future. This has been proved over and over again by the quantities of simple bygones that are now considered desirable antiques.

For example, locks and keys and other fixtures and fittings such as door knobs, knockers and shop fittings of many kinds are all collectable. As the age of supermarkets takes over from individual shops, when demolition is in progress it is sometimes possible to obtain interesting souvenirs very cheaply on the site before the bulldozers get to work and the excavated material is ground to powder. Old houses and cottages disappear overnight and in them there are likely to be mementoes of the past which would be well worth saving to add to your collection.

On page 146 is illustrated an example of a Fire Mark still occasionally to be seen fixed to the wall of old cottages, houses or shops. These quaint little lead or metal plaques, showing a variety of devices, were originally issued by fire insurance offices which ran their own brigades to deal with fires, serving only their own policy holders. Small Fire Marks were attached to the walls of insured buildings and carried the emblem of their company to identify the premises for the firemen concerned, many of whom in those far off days could not read, so their company's insured buildings were easily recognisable to them by these pictorial marks. It was, of course, not a really practical method as fire spreads rapidly and the various insurance companies soon made reciprocal arrangements so that the first firemen to arrive on the scene dealt with the flames, whatever company's sign marked the blazing building.

1. *A Fire Mark attributed to an insurance company known as Salamander operating during the years 1822–1835. From the loan collection at a Chelsea Antiques Fair*

Before the Great Fire of London, fire insurance was unknown and it is believed that the first fire insurance policy was issued in 1667, the year after this appalling disaster. This was such a new idea that it was slow to be accepted by the

2. *A selection of Continental keys. From the left, Italian, early 17th-century. French, 18th century. Italian, 19th century. French, late 17th century. French, circa 1700. From the Peter Phillips collection of antique locks and keys displayed at a recent Chelsea Antiques Fair*

public, but it began to spread and a number of companies were established, all with their individual signs. By 1830 more than a hundred fire offices were in existence, with a wide variety of marks; actually five hundred devices are known which are now enthusiastically collected. Most of them were made of iron or lead, and the earliest examples have the policy number on the base. This practice was later stopped, but if a numbered fire mark is found, it is likely to be an early example. There is now a Fire Mark Circle in existence to help collectors, and the address of the Secretary is 99 North End Road, London NW11.

Locks, keys and padlocks are fascinating and decorative collectors' items, so if a church or other old public building is to be demolished in an area, it is worth asking the foreman on the site if there are any available, as most locks have completely changed in character during the last fifty years or more.

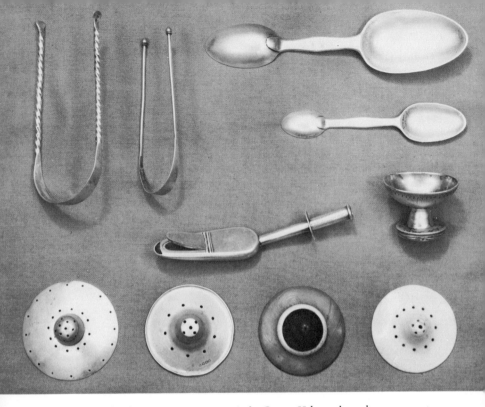

*3. Medical antiques.* From top left, *George II bow-shaped tongue scraper; tongue scraper; double-ended medicine spoon; smaller medicine spoon; rare George III eye cup; William IV Castor Oil spoon with opening flap; nipple shields, George III and IV silver*

At a recent Chelsea Antiques Fair there was an exhibition from a private collection of medical antiques, some of which were of great interest, and illustrated above is a small selection of these. There is no doubt that medical, chemical and veterinary equipment of all kinds is constantly changing, and therefore much of it gets discarded, giving collectors who are interested in such objects a wide opportunity to acquire additional items, at comparatively reasonable prices, unless of course, like those illustrated here, they are already genuine antiques, that is, over a hundred years old. The last hundred years has seen many changes in medical science, and in the equipment of old chemists' shops, which used to have an almost magical display of lovely coloured jars and bottles from which the dispensing was done, on the premises. Nowadays

4. *Students at work on the conservation and restoration of antiques in their workshop at the West Dean College, Chichester, Sussex*

patent medicines and drugs are usually pre-packed and labelled, so any collector who notices a long established chemist having alterations done to his shop would be wise to ask if there are any old items or fixtures for sale, before the demolition squad arrives to transform the premises into a modern chemical supermarket.

Unfortunately many interesting old works of art of all kinds have been lost to posterity through the centuries for want of conservation and repair. Many of the old skills of restoration are in danger of dying out today, and the British Antique Dealers' Association being anxious to arrest this trend, set up a course in conjunction with West Dean College in Sussex, where craftsmen could be trained in the preservation of antique furniture, and another course on the restoration of antique clocks. These are both vital matters, and it is hoped to extend the courses to cover a wide range of related subjects.

West Dean College is a large country mansion which has been converted into some eighty students' study/bedrooms, and is part of the Edward James Foundation created in 1964. The restoration courses are open to students who can show that they are skilled with their hands, are keenly interested in antique furniture or old clocks, and would get deep satisfaction from the ability to restore and conserve old pieces. So often fine furniture is ruined by incompetent work and it is then impossible to conserve or restore. Although it is not envisaged that a year's course will produce master-craftsmen, a foundation of knowledge and experience can be laid and an able student will be taught how things should be done, and equally important, how they should not be done, to detract from the beauty and value of an old piece.

Particulars of these courses can be obtained on request from the Secretary of The British Antique Dealers' Association, 20 Rutland Gate, London, SW7 1BD.

Another interesting activity taking place in Sussex is the Graffham Weavers at Glasses Barn, near Petworth, a centre for the weaving of hand-made floor rugs that are suitable with any decor whether antique or contemporary. These rugs should wear for generations to come and so, no doubt, will one day be recorded as antiques. Hand-weaving is a craft which is reviving in Britain and the rugs woven by Miss Barbara Mullins, who runs Graffham Weavers with other skilled workers, are of a very high standard of craftsmanship and design. All the wool used there is of the finest quality and much of it is dyed by hand on the premises from vegetable dyes made from local woodland plants. In addition to rugs, the Graffham Weavers make bedspreads, hangings, cushions, capes and ponchos which are all of outstanding quality. There are, of course, other well-known centres for hand-weaving in Scotland and in other parts of the British Isles, so collectors may like to

5. *A rug woven by Barbara Mullins of Graffham Weavers, Sussex*

6. *All-purpose mugs from Wedgwood and Sons Ltd designed by Susie Cooper*

consider the merit of their work too, and especially its lasting quality, as hand-woven pure woollen fabrics are becoming scarcer and being replaced with man-made fibres.

Much of today's manufacture of fine chinaware will undoubtedly become future antiques. Historic houses such as Wedgwood, Royal Worcester, Spode, Minton, Royal Doulton, Crown Derby and others all continue to produce the finest quality tableware and ornamental objects in porcelain, bone china, Jasper and other similar materials. The ceramic industry in Britain has a traditional reputation to uphold and their present-day products compare favourably with some of the most fabulous antique pieces of past centuries. Without doubt much of today's superb chinaware will survive to become antiques for the future, and meanwhile give satisfaction to discerning collectors.

# 15 TRANSPORT AND COMMUNICATIONS

During the last hundred years transport and communications have undergone some of the most revolutionary and rapid changes in history, causing a dramatic impact on the life of this planet.

As these changes have taken place and the old ways have been overtaken by the new inventions, a ready demand has grown up for mementoes of this nostalgic past. For example, horse drawn vehicles have largely disappeared from the roads and off the land, with the result that carriage lamps, horse brasses and old harness of all kinds have become desirable collectors' items. Many horse drawn vehicles such as farm carts, ploughs, coaches, carriages, gigs and traps are now interesting museum pieces, while their place in the working world has been taken over first by steam, and then by the internal combustion engine and motor vehicles of all kinds. Almost before the world had become accustomed to these drastic innovations, the aeroplane roared overhead and speed took on a new dimension.

The old canals, with their colourful, horse-drawn narrow boats, which once linked our industrial towns, gave way to the railways, which in turn lost ground to motor transport and air travel, leaving picturesque memories and souvenirs behind. The Waterways Museum at Stoke Bruerne near Towcester in Northamptonshire on the banks of the Grand Union Canal, takes an affectionate look backwards to the heyday of the canal era and the exhibits are a splendid selection of boat relics, brasses, traditional boat-folk possessions and costumes, which make the past come vividly alive. In addition there are quan-

1. *The Birmingham 'Tally-Ho' coaches passing 'The Crown' at Hollo-way. A coloured aquatint after Pollard's oil painting of 1826*

2. *A selection of antique horse brasses*

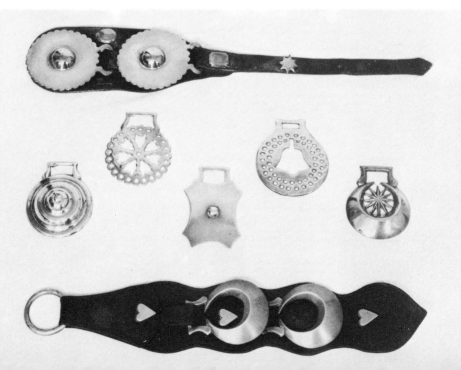

tities of prints, photographs, maps, documents, locks, pad-locks and keys and innumerable other mementoes of canal life in the nineteenth century.

Some of the old crafts have survived and there is a souvenir shop near the museum where there is a good selection of decorative and typical painted tin-ware objects, as used on the narrow boats, and these are for sale; but old pieces of painted tin-ware and canal relics are becoming very scarce.

1975 has seen a number of British Rail celebrations of 150 years of passenger transport, culminating in the opening of a fine Railway Museum at Stockton in Yorkshire, where old steam locomotives and equipment are now in noble retirement. Railwayana of all kinds is most collectable today – but

3. *A gaily painted 'steamer' and her crew on a canal in* 1900

what of the future? If the air is to take over completely from land transport, relics of the diesel age and electric trains may one day become valuable antiques. The change from steam has been drastic and with the closure of so many railway stations and branch lines opportunities for souvenir hunters and collectors in recent years have been plentiful.

4. *Some collectable old railway relics*

Old maps and sea charts are very collectable and give an interesting insight into the way of life through the centuries. For example, the illustration on page 158 shows a part of one of the earliest road maps, which was the work of John Ogilby. It took him years of study and labour to produce the first volume of his now famous work and unfortunately he died in 1676 before completing the other volumes. His ingenious maps showed the main roads from one city to another in parallel strip form, and included such quaint details as a mound when the road ran uphill and an inverted mound when it ran downhill. Each road was mapped with great skill and were the first to adopt the standard mile. They were carefully measured with a 'way wiser' or measuring wheel, a modern version of which is still used for road measurement today.

It cannot be stressed too strongly, however, that a collector of old maps should beware of reproductions of which there are quantities on the market. It is wise to consult an expert as to what to look for if authentic examples are required. Roger Baynton-Williams has recently written a book entitled *Investing in Maps* and he is a well-known and approachable authority on the subject.

It is as well to remember that with the age of motorways, maps made prior to the last twenty years are likely to be out of date already and may well become antiques for the future.

Vintage cars need no introduction. The one illustrated on page 159 emphasises the rapid change of fashion and design in the motoring world. Motoring relics such as mascots are now out of date but very collectable. The sale of motoring mascots at Christie's in 1975 illustrated the value placed upon these charming little mementoes. I feel the lush brochures of prestige motor cars available in dealers' showrooms may also be collectors' items in the future.

Under the heading of 'communications' one could well consider television and radio, and already there are collectors of old sets of both mediums. These also are constantly chang-

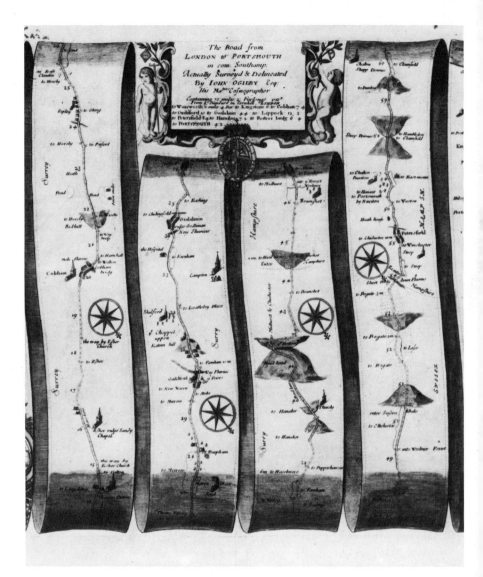

5. and 6. Above, *John Ogilby's road map was one of the earliest produced, circa 1675. This shows a section of the map and the method he used to show undulations in the road.* Right, *the famous 30/98 Vauxhall generally regarded as the first British sports car. It was built before 1914*

ing and might be worthy of consideration for a would-be collector.

Postal relics of all kinds through the ages are of course very collectable indeed, including first day stamps, and other forms of philately too numerous to mention, but these can open up a whole new sphere of interest in this ever-changing world, and are likely to increase in value.

Souvenirs of air travel too, are legion; in fact a discriminating collector has a wide field of transport relics of all kinds from which to make an interesting choice without necessarily involving much expense – so good hunting!

7. *'Bird in Flight', a motoring mascot of the 1930s*

# 16 PUB SIGNS, TRADE SYMBOLS, USEFUL SHOPS AND MUSEUMS

The English 'pubs' started as resting places for pilgrims, and they have maintained a reputation for friendliness and welcome since the time of Chaucer. As the smaller brewers are taken over by large national combines, however, the gaily painted inn signs of the past are fast disappearing, which is tragic, as they represent now an almost extinct folk art.

The same can be said of shop signs which were useful when large numbers of the public could not read. For example when Chippendale opened his workshop in London it was identified outside by the sign of 'The Chair', and shop signs showing objects symbolic of their trades were indispensable in city life. As education became general these were less needed, and the names of shopkeepers and their wares replaced the carved symbolic signs, which are now becoming rare collectors' items. Old shop fittings, however, are worth considering today, especially such items as 'By Royal Appointment' signs. The old pawnbrokers' signs of three golden balls, so plentiful before the 1939 war, are now becoming rare as the welfare state mercifully makes the demand for a pawnbroker's services less frequent. However, some of these signs still exist, in old city streets where the barber's red and white pole is also occasionally seen, but the recent demolition of our old city centres has deprived us of many decorative and often humorous shop signs, and turned them into collectors' items.

The system of numbering houses and shops and naming the streets, which took place during the eighteenth and nineteenth centuries, also caused many interesting and amusing signs to disappear. Christopher Sykes Antiques of Market

Place in Woburn, Bedfordshire, has a large and valuable collection of tavern or pub signs, also trade symbols, and it is well worth a visit, as this is a very specialised subject and some items in his collection are for sale. Mr Sykes is an expert on the origin and whole subject of old pub and shop signs, both of which have long and romantic histories. The modern pub has either no painted sign or symbol swinging in the breeze, or has possibly been re-named in the modern idiom, as illustrated opposite, with similar subjects for their signs to 'The Machine Man'. Old painted mirror signs have been much collected, but many reproductions of these have recently flooded the market. Tankards of all ages are collectable and mementoes of character from inns and pubs are likely to become valuable.

Asprey's of Bond Street, recently became aware of the demand for inn signs, but realised that most of them are uncomfortably large for the average collector and so produced some fine small reproductions which are illustrated on page 164. These are made in silver and enamel, thereby preserving the original designs of historic old 'pubs' but in miniature. Many lovely things that will no doubt become antiques for the future are available from Asprey's. They distribute luxury merchandise of many kinds and have their own silversmiths with workshops on the premises, in addition to a good selection of antiques. Their hardstone carvings and silverware, contemporary gold articles and general gifts, are all fabulous of their kind, expressing luxury and elegance, qualities which, alas, are becoming rarer as the years pass by. The far-seeing and discriminating collector will see a wide variety of lovely objects in luxury shops such as Asprey's and Garrards of Regent Street – objects which will doubtless be of even greater value in a hundred years from now.

Most antique shops these days specialise in some particular merchandise. For example, furniture of a special period, antique jewellery, porcelain, oriental antiques, paintings, prints, maps, and so on, although there are still a number of general antique dealers to be found. A collector of any special

1. *Pub signs including an unusual modern coloured one showing a metal robot against a bright blue sky*

1. *Shop signs used by tobacconists. Left, a rare 18th century carved wood Blackamore figure.* **Right,** *the figure is holding a spiral roll of tobacco*

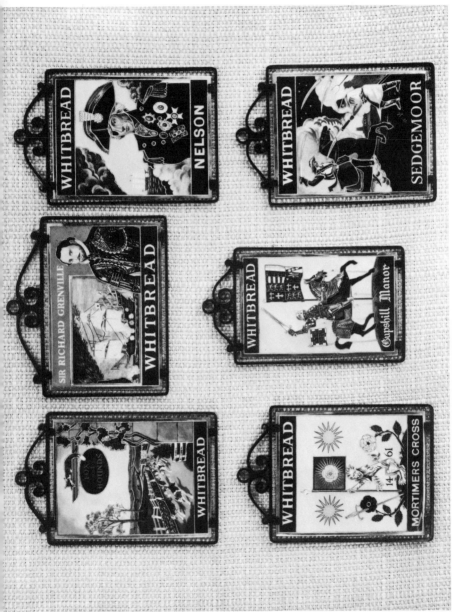

3. Six well-known Inn signs reproduced in miniature

subject is, of course, wise to enlist the help and co-opera-
tion of an expert who specialises in the items he seeks, and
a great deal can be learned by beginner collectors in such con-
sultations. Most good dealers will be found friendly and
helpful to a would-be collector who is also an enquirer, and
there is still an atmosphere of leisure and courteous consideration to be found in the antique trade. Perhaps it is
dealing with beautiful things that maintains this old-world
courtesy.

For a wide selection of general antiques and small furniture
a most useful and helpful concern is the Stately Antiques
Market at Woburn Abbey, which is housed in the fine stable
block of this lovely venue, and it consists of over fifty small
shops belonging to antique dealers from many parts of the
country. It claims to be the largest antiques centre out of
London, and is open every day of the week, including Sun-
days. There are, of course, many antiques markets throughout
Britain, and space permits only very few examples here as a
possible guide to collectors.

Craft shops are opening in towns and villages all over
Britain which offer for sale quantities of interesting studio
pottery, carvings, paintings, hand-made jewellery, weaving,
engraved glass and many other fascinating objects. Here again
the discriminating collector may find some work by a young
artist on his way to fame and fortune, which may well increase
in value as his or her reputation grows. The early works of
many now famous artist-craftsmen fetch high prices at auction
today.

One of the recently founded craft shops is at the Victoria
and Albert Museum which opened in 1974 and is now very
successful. Craftsmen and women are at last receiving well-
deserved recognition in the world of fine art, and the government sponsored Design Centre in the Haymarket, London,
and the Crafts Advisory Committee and Gallery at Waterloo
Place, London, have done much to foster their work during
the last decade. They have brought it to the notice of the

public with the help of exhibitions, as well as by indexing the names and addresses of all registered craftsmen and women and making these indexes available for reference at both Centres.

There has also been recognition and a revival of rural crafts, such as thatching, basket-making, hand-made lace, saddlery, bookbinding, weaving, wood-turning, wrought-iron work, hand-made furniture and decorative wheel-thrown pottery. Here again government support has encouraged training schemes, evening classes and exhibitions through the 'Country Workshops' sponsored by the Rural Industries Bureau, 35 Camp Road, Wimbledon Common, London, SW19. They publish an annual booklet *Country Workshops* which lists many country workshops throughout the British Isles. Smaller crafts have also received encouragement through the same organisation, and one has but to glance through the booklet – which also gives details of retail crafts shops – to realise the wealth of talent that exists in the countryside today.

An interesting revival has recently taken place of the old craft of enamelling exquisite trifles, similar to those made between 1750 and 1840, which were generally known as 'Battersea Enamels'. Many of these were made in the Midlands as well as London and the proprietor of a unique gift shop, Halcyon Days of Brook Street in London, has always been particularly fascinated by these antique enamel snuff boxes and other exquisite luxury items so popular with the Georgian and French aristocracy of the eighteenth and early nineteenth centuries. The industry declined in the nineteenth century when the Industrial Revolution caused labour to drift from small specialist workshops into big new factories, with the resulting loss of skills requiring dedicated handwork.

Enamelling on copper, one of the most endearing crafts in England, had virtually ceased to exist by the late 1830s. In 1968 a chance encounter between Halcyon Days and a small firm of enamellers in Bilston led to a venture which now produces exquisite small enamel boxes, eggs, and other small

4. *Part of the Woburn Abbey Antiques Centre, Bedfordshire, showing two of the small shops*

objects beautifully decorated in colour by commissioned artists, in the eighteenth century tradition, but with the designs now usually commemorating some present-day event or anniversary. An example of these superb little boxes is illustrated below. Some are made in limited editions and they are all most collectable and beautiful little treasures.

Many books are published to help would-be collectors with their studies, but visits to museums are an essential source of information, and *Museums and Galleries in Great Britain* which is published every year by Index Publishers in Bedfordshire, is invaluable, as it includes alphabetical lists of museums, art galleries, etc. throughout Britain under subjects and geo-

*5. The Jane Austen Bicentenary enamel box decorated in deep pink with charcoal lettering. An oval box size 2⅛"*

graphical locations, in addition to a useful list of service and regimental museums. It also describes some specialised museums, such as Claverton Manor near Bath, the American Museum in Britain, with its fabulous collection of American antiques; the Wellcome Institute of the History of Medicine in London; the Jewish Museum, where treasured Jewish antiquities are housed; and countless other important museums, as well as listing the smaller local museums throughout this country that hold so much of interest.

Perhaps it is not generally realised how helpful museums can be in identifying personal antiques or inherited treasures for members of the public. The large national museums such

*6. One of the parlours furnished with American antiques in The American Museum at Claverton Manor, Bath*

as the British Museum, the Victoria and Albert Museum and
the National Gallery and Portrait Gallery, all have special
times each week for this free specialised service. It would be as
well, therefore, to telephone and enquire for these times and
particulars before making a long journey to consult their
experts. Local museums can also be helpful with advice on
identification, but museums, of course, never advise on valuations.

The principal London Auction Rooms, such as Christie's
and Sotheby's will advise as to a suitable reserve price for any
object that might be considered for auction. This service is
free and without obligation to sell your treasures. It can be
most helpful as a guide for such purposes as insurance. Actual
valuations for insurance of art treasures can also be arranged
by them.

The word 'antique' is now applied to objects of many
periods, but the British Antique Dealers' Association recently
stated that description can only genuinely be used to describe
articles made at least a hundred or more years ago. One
hundred and thirty years old was once the laid down margin,
so this concession has released many Victorian objects on to
the collectors' market. BADA was formed in 1918 and since
its inception has watched over and protected the antique trade
in Britain, and now has also a number of members overseas. It
has done much to put the trade on a professional footing, and
is now one of the finest administrative bodies in the world of
Fine Arts. The main qualifications for membership are integ-
rity and expert knowledge. The quality of a member's stock is
also taken into consideration, and these qualifications for
membership of every member are reviewed annually by the
Council. The well-known BADA sign displayed in the shop
window of an antique dealer is indeed a recommendation of
good service. The headquarters of the Association is at 20
Rutland Gate, London, SW7, and a list of their many members throughout the British Isles, the USA and the Common-
wealth is published annually in booklet form and is available

to all members, or by post on application to the Secretary.

Antiques by their very existence take our thoughts back to earlier days and to visualising a different way of life. In these pages we have endeavoured also to look forward, to build up our present collections with precious, interesting or curious objects, anticipating the time when the 1970s have passed into history. Art inevitably tells its own tale about the era of its inception and becomes a true expression of its times. The present space age is surely an era when growing recognition of the infinite beauty and variety of natural forms are ever opening up new vistas and interests for the years to come; it is therefore hoped and anticipated that in one hundred years from now the creative visual arts of the seventies will be looked upon as fabulous antiques.

# BIBLIOGRAPHY

There are so many fine books written on collecting and art subjects, and space here permits me only to mention a few to which I have referred in my text. If some of these prove to be out of print they can usually be obtained for study in reference sections at Public Libraries.

*Ecclesiastical Embroidery* by Beryl Dean
*Wall Hangings Today* by Vera Sherman. Published by Mills and Boon
*A Potter's Book* and *The Potter's Challenge* by Bernard Leach
*Collecting British Banknotes* by Colin Narbeth. Published by Stanley Gibbons
*The Picture Postcard and Its Origins* and *The Valentine and Its Origins* by Frank R. Staff
*Buttons for the Collector* by P. Peacock
*Collecting Playing Cards* by S. Mann
*Investing in Maps* by Roger Baynton-Williams. Published by Barrie and Jenkins
*Country Workshops* published by Rural Industries Bureau, 35 Camp Road, Wimbledon Common
*Kitchen Antiques* by Mary Norwak. Published by Ward Lock.
List of BADA Members obtainable from 20 Rutland Gate, London, SW7
*Museums and Galleries in Great Britain* published by Index Publishers, Dunstable, Bedfordshire

# INDEX